For Peter F.

founder of the Comp

and its director, 1956   09

Contents

Prayer as Night Falls

The Compline Choir at St. Mark's Cathedral, Seattle   Gabrielle Fine, 2009

1

Compline in the Holy Box

AN INTRODUCTION

There was something numinous in the experience. I felt so strongly around me the presence of God. I knew I was sharing in something with these young people. I knew they had come—been drawn there, in the hope and expectation of an encounter with the Holy. And so it was. In that darkened Cathedral, I felt, once again, the presence of God.

—EDMOND BROWNING[1]

* * *

As I remember, it was the first weekend in October 1964 when David introduced me to Compline. We drove in his VW Beetle from Tacoma, where I had just begun college, to Seattle, about thirty miles to the north. Eventually we arrived at the top of Capitol Hill, and I saw for the first time our destination—the great concrete hulk of St. Mark's Cathedral. I was eighteen, a music student. Dave, whom I had just met the week before, sang the ancient service of Compline every Sunday night, and suggested I try it out.

Compline is what monks and nuns pray every day before they go to sleep. In many monasteries, after Compline they keep the Great Silence—no sounds until the early hours of the morning, when they chant "O Lord, open my lips, and my mouth will proclaim your praise."[2] Their silence broken, they begin the daily cycle of prayer called the "offices" or the Divine Hours. There are as many as eight of these offices, and Compline (from the Latin word *Completorium*) completes the cycle.

✳   ✳   ✳

We parked in the cathedral lot and admired the commanding view to the west: the twinkling lights of houses on Seattle's Queen Anne Hill, the famous Space Needle, where I had gone to the World's Fair two years before, and at their feet, Lake Union, a freshwater lake connected by channels and locks to the saltwater Puget Sound.

I was full of the excitement of the last few weeks—freshman orientation, dorm life, new friends and studies, and teaching Sunday school in a Methodist church in a shabby corner of Tacoma, which was where I met Dave, an alum of my university, who was playing a Bach fugue after church on the little electric organ. We talked about music, and Dave invited me to join him the next week to sing Compline.

In the spring of 1956, Peter Hallock, the organist/ choirmaster of St. Mark's Episcopal Cathedral, Seattle, invited a group of men to sing the Office of Compline every Sunday night. They sang from a little booklet with the original chants from medieval times, adapted to words approved by the Church of England in the late 1920s. Hallock, who grew up in Kent, Washington, had experienced Compline at Episcopal Church camps and retreats in the 1930s. After serving in World War II, he studied organ and composition at the University of Washington in Seattle, and then attended the Royal School of Church Music from 1949–51 at Canterbury, where he sang from the Order of Compline, which he brought back with him to his first job at St. Mark's.

After rehearsing the chants in an outbuilding that served as a temporary choir room, the little singing club (once-a-week monks?) would move into the empty cathedral, where the spacious acoustics made the chant come alive. At this time, to hear Compline sung outside a monastery would have been uncommon enough, but hearing it sung in English—an absolute rarity.

✳ ✳ ✳

Dave introduced me to Peter Hallock, a slender man of about forty, bright and friendly, with a hint of British reserve; finding I was a tenor, he invited me to sit behind a choir desk in the second row. There were also "countertenors"— men who sang in falsetto, allowing them to sing as high as women altos—an idea that was totally novel to me at the time. They sat in the first row, and baritones and basses sat in the third. We started rehearsing a psalm from a thin hardbound Psalter. Mrs. Andrews, a stout woman in her eighties who spoke in a lilting way (I had never heard a "Welsh" accent), brought us tea in china cups on a big tray. She offered sugar and milk, but, being unfamiliar with the British custom, I only took a couple lumps of sugar. I rested my cup on the shelf under my desk, careful not to spill on my music.

As the group continued to meet, they occasionally added a polyphonic anthem to the service, and Hallock began to compose his own pieces—but in those days before photocopiers, it was a tedious process to reproduce unpublished works. In November 1956, Hallock put an announcement in the parish bulletin, inviting anyone who wanted to attend "Compline" to come on Sunday evenings at 10 PM. Only a few people showed up—the same was true the following year, when the service time was moved up to 9:30. Not that attendance was a primary objective—the choir joked about people out there "ruining the acoustics." In 1962, one of the announcers for KING-FM, a Seattle classical music station, thought it would be interesting to broadcast the service live from St. Mark's. The owner of KING Broadcasting, Dorothy S. Bullitt, was a friend of John C. Leffler, Dean of St. Mark's, and soon a dedicated phone line was installed; the weekly live broadcast of the Compline Service began to attract an audience.

✳   ✳   ✳

I was given a choir robe to wear—a long purple thing like a nightgown that buttoned down the front. We lined up in a space called the "Chantry," which was inside the cathedral, open to the ceiling above, but enclosed on three sides by a wooden wall about twelve feet high. There were two large doors that opened out into the cathedral, and we processed in single file to the northeastern corner, where there were three choir desks arranged in a semicircle. The immensity of the space overwhelmed me—the wooden-beamed ceiling ninety or a hundred feet above, the four huge columns—a cavern that seemed even larger in the darkness. It was hard to tell in the dim light, but there were about twenty or thirty people sitting on pews or kneeling, waiting for us to begin.

Construction began on St. Mark's in 1928. It was designed as a Gothic layer cake—a central cubic core a hundred feet high, with a smaller second layer, half as wide, but 150 feet high—creating a vast tower void when viewed from below. However, a year after work started the Great Depression intervened, and elaborate plans had to be curtailed—no tower, no added transepts (the wings that give a church its cruciform shape). What remained was the original cube, the largest concrete pour in the state of Washington until

Grand Coulee Dam was finished in 1941. After its dedication, St. Mark's Cathedral was aptly named "The Holy Box."[3]

✳ ✳ ✳

Winfield Tudor, a countertenor from Barbados, clasped a small transistor radio to his ear. His job was to listen to KING-FM, and when he heard the Compline service announced, he pointed to Charles Sherwood, a fiftyish tenor, who projected in perfect Shakespearian tones an opening prayer that began "Beloved in Christ, let us make this church glad with our songs of praise." We then began an orison, a "sung prayer":

> *Now the day is over,*
> *Night is drawing nigh,*
> *Shadows of the evening*
> *Steal across the sky.*

Our tones resounded in the darkness, drifting out to play in the beamed ceiling and then return to us. I noticed a large open space to my left in the newly remodeled east wall, which I was told would eventually hold an enormous pipe organ. My own song went out into this mysterious cavern of darkness. What were we doing? We were singing about the darkness, in the darkness, to the darkness. . . .:

> *Jesus, give the weary*
> *Calm and sweet repose;*
> *With Thy tend'rest blessing*
> *May our eyelids close.*

I felt a catch in my throat and a tearing-up—I reined in my emotions, and went on singing. The third verse was pianissimo, *very softly:*

> Through the long night watches
> May Thine angels spread
> Their white wings above me,
> Watching round my bed.

It was a child's prayer—"Now I lay me down to sleep"—but here were men in their fifties singing this in utmost sincerity and sweetness.

After that first night, singing Compline in the Holy Box became the high point of my week. An experience both artistic and social drew me at first—a deep encounter with beauty, and the bonding of a group whose weekly goal was to put together, in a short rehearsal, a sung prayer service suitable for live radio. Compline, a ritual at the close of the day poised between light and darkness, and our Sunday-night observance, became a part of my weekly natural rhythm. Then there were the qualities of peace and calm repose that followed from the recitation of a monastic office—a sacred time of prayer, reflection, and meditation—a refuge from the hectic world of school or work.

A few years later, during the hippie-proclaimed "Summer of Love" in 1967, hundreds of people, mostly young like me, began coming to our service. Partly due to the difficulty of finding a seat, or for the opportunity to make a countercultural statement, many attendees sat or even reclined on the floor or the steps to the altar—looking very much like the crowds at the San Francisco park gatherings, or perhaps the Beatles meditating on their trip to India. By then, I had a growing sense of ministry in what we were doing—another reason for returning to Compline each week.

The popularity of the service in Seattle did not go unnoticed, and the interest generated among both Lutherans and Episcopalians led to the inclusion of an Order of Compline in their new prayer books published at the end of the 1970s.[4] Choirs outside Seattle started Compline services— in Honolulu and Pittsburgh, Austin and Minneapolis and Vancouver—many groups founded by directors who had first heard the service or had sung in the choir in Seattle. As these mainline Protestant churches discovered Compline, the Roman Catholic Church continued its post–Vatican II reform of the Divine Office, and most monasteries and seminaries in the United States set aside their Latin chant books and began to write music for new Orders of Compline, renamed "Night Prayer." Since the 1970s, the number of organized groups outside of monasteries who sing or say Compline has multiplied; today there are over fifty groups with websites across the United States and Canada that offer Compline services, and over one hundred Facebook groups that contain the name.

The Compline phenomenon was one of the precursors to a resurgence of interest in contemplative spirituality during the last half of the twentieth century. It was stimulated not only by an increased knowledge of Eastern religions but also by a rediscovery of Christian monastic and mystical traditions, including the daily cycle of fixed-hour prayer. Contemplative spirituality is expressed today in other ways (Centering Prayer, *lectio divina*, chant, and silent meditation), but many Christians outside the monastery are now praying one or two of the offices on a regular basis.

Since the mid-1960s I have witnessed the hundreds who attend our service every Sunday evening in person, filling the pews or reclining on the floor in that tradition of informality unique to Seattle Compline.[5] I think also of the thousands who listen to the live broadcast, or hear it later over the Internet.[6] Those who come in person arrive—sometimes in whole busloads—from various churches, from many different Christian communities as well as those who would call themselves "spiritual but not religious." They include fundamentalists and agnostics, evangelicals and aging "New Agers" who come together to partake in something that comes out of ancient liturgical traditions.[7] They have a need, unmet by other religious experiences, for silence, for the absence of preaching, for no other participation than a kind of "active listening." They have, quite simply, a hunger for direct, unmediated experience of the Divine Presence. As Peter Hallock wrote once—"These are people engaged in the business of knowing God."[8]

I'm somewhat amazed to relate that I am still singing with the Compline Choir at St. Mark's in Seattle—with all the awe and wonder of the eighteen-year-old kid who started almost fifty years ago. All those things I mentioned that drew me to Compline stir me still. But the sense of ministry I feel about the service we provide—a service where a kind of "sacred space" is made for people in their busy week—is what has prompted me to write this book.

Prayer as Night Falls is the result of my wanting to share memories, reflections, and insights from a spiritual practice that has deepened over decades. I want to share stories, texts, and music that have shaped and formed my own spiritual journey, which I hope will be beneficial to others on their own journeys. And I want to explore the insights that the history and particular nature of Compline might give us. My hope is that you will find things here that will enrich and inspire your spiritual life.

The next chapter will complete our introduction by giving an overview of Compline and describing how it is prayed today throughout the Christian world. Then I will interpose chapters on the story of Compline's development as a ritual over the last two millennia between chapters on six "themes" that arise from Compline itself or are significant to me from my experience. Here, in the order they are presented, are these ideas and the qualities of the spiritual life they evoke for me.

Darkness and Light! Practicing Vigilance

The Office of Compline refers many times to the contrasts symbolized by light and darkness; among these are good and evil, or knowledge and ignorance. The dangers of the night come with the darkness, and salvation comes with the dawn. Inner darkness is alienation from God and entrapment in false pursuits; enlightenment is the finding of our true selves. In our spiritual journey we must be alert and awake both to the significance of experience and to the choices between light and darkness with which we are presented every day.

Death and Life: Accepting Mortality

The image of sleep as a "little death" stirs us to contemplate our own end—the Office of Compline underscores this with the response "Into your hands I commend my spirit" and the canticle "Lord, let your servant depart in peace." We need to prepare for death, to "number our days," that through knowledge of our relationship to this life and its divine source, we may come to an acceptance and an embracing of our lives, including our life's end.

Compline and the Mystic Path: Seeking the Eternal

In praying a monastic office, we enter into sacred time, where our attention is entirely in the present moment, but where past and future are contained as well. Through prayer, contemplation, and silence, we enter into an inner sacred space where communion is found with the Divine Presence.

Such mystical encounters strengthen our relationship with the divine and increase attunement on our own spiritual journey.

Beauty: Seeking Good

The process of making sacred music has made me keenly aware of the relationship of beauty to divine truth, and the role of the artist in giving us glimpses of the Divine Presence. We need such experiences to counter the noise and stress of our present time, as well as all that is a source of fear and anxiety. Encounters with beauty bring us closer to everything that is good, and strengthen our inner love of harmony and quality in our work and relationships. We learn to appreciate the beautiful, and to become "artists" in the creation of our daily lives, which is simply revealing God working in us and through us.

Community: Practicing Compassion

We all belong to communities: families, groups, nations, world. In singing the Office of Compline, I have been part of a special community of those with whom I make music and, in a broader sense, with those for whom we offer the service. Even the contributions of those who have been a part of our work and passed on remain in the culture and fabric of our communal life. As we deepen our relationship with God, finding our true selves, we realize that we are one with our brothers and sisters, growing in compassion, inclusiveness, and hospitality.

Finding Lasting Peace: Putting It All Together

From the Office of Compline comes the last but perhaps most important theme, the transformation of the soul toward *inner peace*. Released from fear, we are protected and safe through the emptying of ourselves in meditation, through faith and acceptance of our life/death, through compassion for others. Through Compline we find the protection we sought, not from some remote deity, but from the divine manifested within ourselves and in all of creation.

To illustrate and make the contents of this book more present to you, I've collected some texts and music that have been exemplary for me from the hundreds of selections sung or spoken at our service over the years. At the website www. prayerasnightfalls.com, you may listen to these selections at the time you read about them, or whenever you like. After you finish this chapter, for example, you may want to hear what an entire Compline service sounds like, in which case you can listen to example 1 on the website and follow along with the text of the Order of Compline in appendix A. Whenever I mention a particular example in the book, I will have a little note like this: (Listen: example 1). The full texts of the examples may be found either on the website or in appendix B. And if you want to know more about praying the Divine

Hours or Compline in particular, appendix C contains a list of selected resources.

Throughout *Prayer as Night Falls*, I've put my own reminiscences in italics, as you have found in this chapter. My hope is that these personal reflections will tie the thoughts or ideas in particular chapters to real, concrete spiritual experiences, making the spirituality of Compline more relevant to you.

And now, let's return briefly back to my first night at Compline.

✳ ✳ ✳

That first night praying Compline, after the orison had been sung, the reader began the office proper: "The Lord Almighty grant us a quiet night and a perfect end." We answered, "Amen."

The reader continued:

> *Beloved in Christ, be sober, be vigilant; because your adversary the devil, as a roaring lion, walketh about, seeking whom he may devour: whom resist, steadfast in the faith. But thou O Lord, have mercy upon us. Thanks be to God.*

The cantor intoned: "O God, make speed to save us." We sang in answer: "O Lord, make haste to help us."

And so Compline began that first night long ago, just like it has every week since. Those first few sentences contain all the main themes of Night Prayer: a call to vigilance and repentance as darkness descends; a prayer for a restful sleep and a peaceful death; and a plea for steadfast faith and for protection within the Divine Presence.

Now your journey with Compline begins. May it be fruitful for you, and bring you peace.

2

Round Me Falls the Night

ELEMENTS OF COMPLINE

The duteous day now closeth,
Each flower and tree reposeth,
Shade creeps o'er wild and wood:
Let us, as night is falling,
On God our Maker calling,
Give thanks to Him, the Giver good.

—PAUL GERHARDT,
Praxis Pietatis Melica, 1648[9]

* * *

A few years ago, my wife and I drove to the western edge of Seattle's Beacon Hill, where we could watch a particularly beautiful sunset. As we admired the colors, my attention was drawn to sounds in the trees behind us. I saw hundreds of crows gathered among the branches, all facing the setting sun.

My first impression was that the crows were having their own Vespers service. I have since learned that ornithologists describe such a gathering as a social time, common to many species of bird, before

heading off to a roosting tree for silence and sleep. But I found it
intriguing that other created beings have a need for a ritual marking
the passing of day into night.

I prayed and sang the Office of Compline for many years without much thought about its special place in Christian prayer. It was enough for me to know that it was said in monasteries before retiring for the night, and I had a vague notion that monks and nuns said a number of these prayer services throughout the day. Had I been a Roman Catholic, I would have known that, outside of monasteries, the offices were said in private by priests, prayed regularly in seminaries, and occasionally at larger churches or cathedrals. If I were an Anglican or Episcopalian, I would have known about Morning and Evening Prayer, but perhaps not their origin in the medieval offices. Growing up in Presbyterian and Methodist churches, I had no idea how many elements in common the offices had with a typical Sunday morning service.

In the 1960s I also didn't know that many specialists in Christian history were interested in bringing back daily prayer at specific times of day into the lives of ordinary people. In the first three centuries of the church, prayer in common, especially in the morning and evening, involved the whole assembly, but with the establishment of freedom from persecution, daily-prayer practice was left to monastics or urban clergy. I had heard of Vatican II and the change within the Catholic Church, but didn't realize that the offices were being transformed into something more compact—the Liturgy of the Hours (1970)—which was designed so that more nonclergy could pray the offices daily.

Almost fifty years later, it seems to me that we have gone through a time similar to the 1500s, when the printing press brought about the re-formation of daily prayer, making it possible for large numbers of people to access the Bible as well as the "breviary," a small prayer book for daily use. Today's communication revolution, the Internet, along with portable devices, has made many versions of daily prayer instantly accessible. And a number of books of and about fixed-hour prayer and the spirituality of the offices have been written, especially in the last twenty-five years.[10]

In this chapter I'd like to provide a framework for the history and spirituality of Compline. I'll discuss its various parts or elements, how it is related to the other offices, and where and how Compline is prayed today.

For 1,400 years, the model set by St. Benedict (d. AD 547) of praying at fixed times of day was the most common method used in the monasteries of Western Christendom. These eight offices are the "classical" form still prayed by many who observe the tradition:

MATINS	in the middle of the night, or in the pre-dawn hours
LAUDS	at sunrise
PRIME	about 6 a.m.
TERCE	mid-morning

SEXT	noon
NONE	mid-afternoon
VESPERS	at sunset
COMPLINE	before retiring

In the classical eight offices, the ones that have the most content are Matins, Lauds, and Vespers. Prime through None are called the "Little Hours" due to their relative brevity, and Compline is almost as short as these, especially in monasteries.

Today, the number of offices prayed daily varies greatly among communities and individuals, but the times most frequently observed are morning, noon, evening, and before retiring. To pray even one of these times of day is to participate in the "Prayer of the Church," the prayer that is constantly being offered around the world at every moment. And on a larger scale, to join in this daily prayer is to experience a closer connection to the other two Abrahamic faiths, Judaism and Islam, and their fixed-hour prayer traditions.

When praying an office, one is aware of the uniqueness of the present moment and the experience of "sacred time." But there are two other aspects of the spirituality of Compline and the other Christian offices that find expression in their various elements. One is the association of each office with the particular time or "season" of the day, each of which has spiritual characteristics that are underscored by certain prayers, hymns, and readings.[11] Compline, for instance, is a meditation on death, a prayer for protection, and for vigilance in the coming night—three themes that are the subjects of later chapters—and you will see how these themes have influenced the elements of the office.

The other spiritual gift of the offices is that each day is uniquely situated in the context of the liturgical year. The various parts of the offices—antiphons before and after the psalms, the psalms themselves, the hymns, and the prayers— change according the day's observance, whether it is a special saint's day or a particular time or season in the year, such as Advent, Lent, or Easter.

Elements of Compline

Most of the parts of Compline are components of the other offices as well, and I will describe how they are both similar to and different from each other. Also, a few forms are unique to Compline, and I will point those out as well. If you haven't listened to the Office of Compline yet, it may be helpful to follow along with the words in appendix A (Listen: example 1).

All the offices start out with some sort of *introduction*, which includes the invocation "O God, come to my assistance; O Lord, make haste to help me" (in the older English version, the first part reads "O God, make speed to save us"). If said or sung in a community, this prayer is responsorial: a single person says the first part, and all say the second part. Some versions of Compline (but not the other offices) also include the responses "The Lord give us a quiet night and peace at the last. Amen," or "Our help is in the name of the Lord. Who made heaven and earth." There may also be a short reading from 1 Peter ("Be sober, be vigilant . . .") or the response "Turn us, then, O God our Saviour. And let thine anger cease from us."

In many versions of Compline, there is a *confession of sins*, which most often comes as part of the introductory portion. This is unique to Compline because of its position at the end of the day's activities.

Common to all the offices is the singing of a *hymn*, which often comes right after the introduction, or sometimes later in the service. A hymn consists of a number of verses or strophes, each of which is sung to the same melody. If Compline is done very simply, the hymn is about the coming night, such as the one most commonly sung: "Before the ending of the day." A hymn appropriate to the particular day or Christian season may also be sung.

Next is the singing of *psalms*. This is the heart of any office, and the number of psalms is mainly what causes the classical offices to differ in length. St. Benedict appointed three psalms to be sung at Compline, and since the office was done in the semidarkness, the same three were always done, probably since they could be sung from memory. The psalms selected—4, 90 (91), and 133 (134)[12]—all speak of the nighttime. When Compline was sung outside the monastery or prayed in private, other psalms for the various weekdays were added, and today psalms appropriate to the given day may be substituted for

Benedict's three, especially if Compline is the only office prayed in a given day. Each verse of a psalm has a two-part structure, which lends itself to singing in particular musical formulas. Also, sometimes special texts called *antiphons* are said or sung before and after each psalm. This is true not only of Compline but also of the other offices.

All the offices have a short *reading* from Scripture. Compline has a limited number of these readings when compared to the other offices, especially Morning Prayer (Lauds), Evening Prayer (Vespers), or Matins. Today, in the Roman Catholic Liturgy of the Hours, the lessons for Matins are now reduced to two, renamed the Office of Readings, and are no longer recited in the middle of the night.

Compline, in its cathedral form, has, like Morning Prayer and Evening Prayer, an element called a *canticle*. This is a poetic passage from the Bible that is not from the book of Psalms, but has a similar structure. Each of the three canticles is associated with a particular person and event in the New Testament (more later about the canticle for Compline):

MORNING PRAYER (Lauds):	Song of Zechariah (Luke 1:68–79)
EVENING PRAYER (Vespers):	Song of Mary (Luke 1:46–55)
NIGHT PRAYER (Compline):	Song of Simeon (Luke 2:29–32)

Other elements common to all the offices are *prayers* and *responses*. The Lord's Prayer and the Apostles' Creed are always said, as well as a special series of prayers that includes one special prayer for the particular day or event. Also, in all the offices there is another response after the short Scripture reading. Two of these responses associated with Compline are "Into your hands, O Lord, I commend my spirit," and "Keep me as the apple of an eye."

Unique to Compline in its Roman Catholic version is the *Antiphon to the Virgin Mary*, or Marian Antiphon. There are four of these texts, sung since the Middle Ages at the end of Compline, at different times during the year. Like the psalm antiphons, they don't have repeated sections. The word "anthem" comes from "antiphon," and it is common in sung versions of Compline, especially in the Anglican tradition, to sing an anthem at the end of Compline that is appropriate to the day.

The *conclusion* of Compline often has the words "We will lie down in peace and take our rest. For it is you, Lord, only, that make us dwell in safety." Then there is a final response: "Let us bless the Lord. Thanks be to God."

Compline Today

Compline, or Night Prayer, may be prayed in a variety of ways, either said or sung, individually or in community. In the Orthodox Church, Compline has several forms, Great Compline and Small Compline, which are prayed in all churches at specific times during the year. Great Compline involves parts for priest, choir, and the whole assembly, while

Small Compline may also be prayed individually. Only in the Orthodox Church is Compline part of the liturgy on a regular basis for all the people.

Other Christian churches may serve Compline weekly, monthly, on special occasions such as Lent, or—in the case of most churches—not at all. But if given, these special services are only attended by some of the congregation. A number of choirs have come into existence, inspired by Seattle's Compline Choir, who sing the service on a periodic basis. Other groups have come out of the collegiate community, such as one at Columbia University that offered Latin Compline in the Sarum Rite, or the regular services of Compline at Stanford Memorial Church. There was, for a while, a group called "Compline NYC," which sang Compline in unusual locations in New York City, even once under a resonant bridge overpass in a quiet park. In addition to our group in Seattle, some groups have broadcast their service, such as the Minnesota Compline Choir.

Of course, the most prevalent forms of participating in Compline are through individual prayer with one's own book or reading device, or by listening attentively or participating in Compline at a monastery or church service such as ours at St. Mark's in Seattle.

And now, with a little more knowledge of what Compline is all about, we can go on to a deeper look at the story and themes of prayer as night falls.

3

At Day's Close

NIGHT IN ANCIENT TIMES

Half our dayes wee passe in the shadowe of the earth, and the
brother of death exacteth a third part of our lives.

—SIR THOMAS BROWNE, N.D.[13]

✳ ✳ ✳

*The bonfire shifted and sent a shower of sparks up into the darkness
of eastern Washington. It was my last night of a week working as a
counselor at a Methodist church camp called "Lazy-F," in the hills
west of Yakima.*

*That summer of 1968 had been full of uncertainty; I can't remember
which came first—college graduation or my draft notice. When I took
the physical exam along with what seemed like a thousand young
men at Pier 91 in Seattle, my high school "football knee" got me a
deferment; it was only then that I realized I had made no plans for
my future.*

*I decided to stay in Tacoma, get a job, and start applying to
graduate schools to study music history. My roommate's father was*

a Methodist minister, who was in charge of the program at Lazy-F
for a week, and drafted us as "Christian soldiers"—a much better
alternative than shipping off to Vietnam.

We were singing the last song of our gathering around the
campfire—followed by a short sermon, closing prayers, and then
bedtime. I had been elected to give the sermon, and for the life of me
I couldn't think of what to say. I listened to the song, wondering if I
could work the words into my speech. It was a spiritual: "All night,
all day, angels watching over me, O Lord; All night, all day, angels
watching over me."

I suddenly knew what I wanted to say. Maybe the prayers I had
sung at Compline over the previous four years were subconsciously
informing me—but I knew that even though we were surrounded by
darkness, and the firelight was dimming and would eventually turn
to ashes, that the Divine Light, Divine Presence would never desert
us, and we would never be alone.

Night in the Ancient World

The story of Compline begins before history itself, in the feelings and responses engendered by the transition from day to night. Today, artificial light is so pervasive that one has to go to the wilderness to experience a kind of heaviness when darkness comes, and perhaps a fear of helplessness and vulnerability. For our ancestors, dangers lurked in the night. After the discovery of fire, the hearth became a gathering place for story and ritual, like the campfire in my summer memory. And at bedtime, individual prayers for protection from inner and outer demons, and for a restful sleep, were surely offered.

From writings in Western history we learn of the belief, before the advent of artificial light, that the night was Satan's realm—manifested in fantastic creatures that through violence, fear, possession, or temptation destroyed the souls of those who ventured out into the unknown darkness.[14] The night was also seen as a time when, safely locked indoors, one could seek solitude and contemplation apart from the distractions and toil of the day. It was a time for invocation of God's protection and visitation by guardian angels since it was generally believed that symptoms of illness got worse after sunset; all the more reason for the saying, "God give you good night."[15]

The ancient world associated particular deities with the night, others with the transition from light to darkness, and yet others with the transition from this world to the next. Egyptians honored Kuk and Kauket, god and goddess of the night and chaos, as well as Nepthys, a goddess of death and the afterlife, who accompanies Ra on his daily journey at dusk into the realm of darkness. The name of the Hindi goddess Ratri is also the common word for night in many Indian languages. The goddesses Nótt (Norse), Nyx (Greek), and Nox (Roman) have left their names in the roots of the Germanic and Latin words for night. In Greek mythology, Erebus was the god of darkness and chaos. For the Maori, Hine-nui-te-po was goddess of night and death, as well as ruler of the underworld. There were nine Lords of the Night in Aztec and Mayan mythology, each ruling a particular night in a nine-day perpetual cycle; but there was also Metztli, Aztec goddess of the moon, night, and agriculture.

Most of the night deities are goddesses and evoke feminine characteristics of the divine: mystery, fertility, and creative energy. Also, the image, common to both Greek and Norse mythology, of the night goddess driving her chariot across the sky, bringing with it the canopy of night and the stars, conjures up the image of the orderly transition from day to night and a sheltering, motherly protection. Breksta, the Lithuanian goddess of the moon and dusk, protects and watches over the world until the dawn. The people of Israel spoke of an aspect of God called Shekhinah—the life-giving presence that moved over the waters at the creation of the world, resting over the tabernacle, and leading them through their night journey by a pillar of fire. Especially in the later mystical traditions of Judaism, Shekhinah is definitely a feminine presence.

In Greek mythology, the goddess Nyx is the mother of the twins Hypnos (Sleep) and Thanatos (Death). The twins are inseparable. There is something about falling asleep that is intimately connected to the deathly realm. This linkage between sleep and death is an important part of reflection and prayer before retiring: a precursor to Compline.

Although we have many accounts of special observances by the Greeks and Romans on certain nights of the year, descriptions of bedtime rituals are lacking. We do know that in Roman homes, rituals would be offered at a shrine near the hearth, which contained the statue of the household *Lar*, or "guardian deity." A play from about 200 BC preserves the following phrase from a night oblation: "Be well ye Immortal Gods, if I have done anything this day to offend You, may You kindly receive this incense in expiation of my mortal error."[16] Examination of conscience is also often an important part of rites at the close of day.

Another theme important to the transition at dusk was the exaltation of the light. An ancient Hindu ritual of light called *arati* dates back to the time of the Vedas (1500–1000 BC), and is still practiced today. Performed at dusk ("a-rati" literally means "before night"), the ceremony includes holding an oil lamp before a particular deity and moving in a circular motion so that light and shadow play over the image. Illumination is regarded as worship, along with offerings of food, incense, and music.[17] In some ceremonies, people take turns moving the light over each other, symbolizing the eternal spark illuminating the body, which is ephemeral and passing away.

Light is a significant aspect of the Shekhinah, the dwelling or resting presence of God, in Judaism. The tradition of closing one's eyes when receiving a blessing comes from the ancient practice of the priest's making a particular gesture by extending the arms with hands facing downward, thumbs touching, hands extended over each other to form a lattice through which the divine light may shine. People close their eyes in order not to be blinded by the light.

The Bedtime Shema

In Judaism, the custom of saying the Shema before retiring may go back to the writing of the Torah itself. It became obligatory during the period in which the Mishnah was compiled, over the course of the first several centuries of the Christian era.[18] The main part of the text, from Deuteronomy, contains the instruction about the proper time of day to recite it (italics are mine):

> Hear, O Israel: The LORD is our God, the LORD alone. You shall love the LORD your God with all your heart, and with all your soul, and with all your might. Keep these words that I am commanding you today in your heart. Recite them to your children and talk about them when you are at home and when you are away, *when you lie down and when you rise.* Bind them as a sign on your hand, fix them as an emblem on your forehead, and write them on the doorposts of your house and on your gates.[19]

Today's version of the Shema, as found in a Jewish prayer book (or Siddur), also contains many psalms, prayers, and scriptural passages that were added and refined over hundreds of years. It is interesting to consider what parts of the ritual (other than the Shema itself) may have antedated the destruction of the temple in AD 70, and were recited in Jesus's own time. The similarities—as well as the differences—between the version of the Shema recited at bedtime with the Office of Compline are very interesting.[20] Here are some that I think are plausible.

Forgiveness of Sins

In most versions, the Bedtime Shema begins with a statement of forgiveness for anyone who has sinned against the one praying. Other versions also add a prayer for forgiveness of one's own sins. It is easy to imagine devout Jews saying this prayer at bedtime during the time of Jesus; it was perhaps familiar to many already when Jesus instructed his followers to say, "Forgive us our sins, as we forgive those who sin against us."

Psalm 90 (91)[21]

Recited immediately after the Shema, this Psalm, with its images of dwelling under "the shadow of the Almighty" and freedom from "any terror by night," is most associated with nightfall. According to the Midrash, this was a psalm of Moses on the day he constructed the Tabernacle. It invokes the Shekhinah, the resting presence of God.

Psalm 3

This Psalm also invokes the protection of God, and has a verse invoking freedom from fear of death: "I lie down and sleep; I wake again, for the Lord sustains me."

Psalm 4:5

This verse, "Tremble then, and do not sin; speak to your heart in silence upon your bed," is recited three times in some versions of the Bedtime Shema. Another passage that may have been recited at bedtime was verses 7–8:

> You have put gladness in my heart, more than when their grain and wine abound.
>
> I will both lie down and sleep in peace; for you alone, O LORD, make me lie down in safety.

Verse 7 is similar to a verse in Deuteronomy 11, which is read at times along with the Shema: "And you will gather in your grain, your wine, and your oil." These connections show why Psalm 4 was later selected to be used at Compline (Listen: example 2).

The Sixty Mighty Ones and the Traditional Blessing

A passage from the Song of Songs (3:7–8) is often recited in the modern Bedtime Shema, describing the "couch of Shlomo," flanked by sixty warriors:

> Look! It is the litter of Solomon! Around it are sixty mighty men of the mighty men of Israel, all equipped with swords and expert in war, each with his sword at his thigh because of alarms by night.

This passage is immediately followed by the traditional blessing from Numbers 6:24–26:

The LORD bless you and keep you; the LORD make his face to shine upon you, and be gracious to you; the LORD lift up his countenance upon you, and give you peace.

In Hebrew, this blessing contains exactly sixty letters, reminding the person praying of the sixty warriors, or perhaps sixty myriads of angels, who will keep watch in the night. A myriad can either be defined as "ten thousand," or "a great number." The passage serves to remind us that, when we close our eyes in slumber, we are protected by numberless ministers of God.

With its plea for forgiveness, protection, and restful sleep, the Bedtime Shema is the closest expression to Compline that we have from ancient times.

FOR FURTHER READING

Bogard, Paul, ed. *Let There Be Night: Testimony on Behalf of the Dark.* Reno, NV: University of Nevada Press, 2008.

Ekirch, A. Roger. *At Day's Close: Night in Times Past.* New York: W. W. Norton, 2005.

Scherman, Rabbi Nosson, trans. *The Complete ArtScroll Siddur: Weekday/Sabbath/Festival.* New York: Mesorah, 1985. Pocket edition, 2011.

Verdon, Jean. *Night in the Middle Ages.* Translated by George Holoch. Notre Dame: University of Notre Dame Press, 2002.

Entry Doors, St. Mark's Cathedral, Seattle   Gabrielle Fine, 2009

4

Be Sober, Be Vigilant

DARKNESS AND LIGHT

From all ill dreams defend our eyes,
From nightly fears and fantasies;
Tread under foot our ghostly foe,
That no pollution we may know.

—Compline Hymn *Te lucis ante terminum*[22]

* * *

In October 1987 I was traveling with a choir on a pilgrimage through England, France, and Italy that concluded with our singing in Rome for a papal audience at St. Peter's Basilica. While in France we spent one night at Solesmes, a Benedictine monastery whose special mission is to publish the official editions of Gregorian chant. A friend and I had just heard the monks chant Compline before heading out to join the rest of our group for dinner at another building several hundred yards from the monastery gate.

Leaving the lighted street, we stepped into an alley whose cobblestones led downhill toward the River Sarthe, and we suddenly found ourselves in the blackness of the French countryside at night. Unsure of where to step and feeling vulnerable in the enclosing gloom, we made our way in the dark as if blind. How thankful we were, after some time, to see the dim lights from the building where our companions were staying!

For a while, I was immersed in the same darkness that was much more pervasive only a century ago, and still exists in the wild when night falls. It was a dramatic reminder of the need for the Compline prayers we had just heard.

Compline stands at the threshold of light and darkness—a "liminal" time as the clear images of the day fade and night approaches with its connection to fear, vulnerability, and evil. Over hundreds of years, light and darkness have been symbols for other pairs of opposites: good and evil, knowledge and ignorance, safety and fear. And so at nightfall it is natural to consider these opposites and respond with awareness, self-examination, and a renewed yearning for right relationships with ourselves and others. As the reading from the First Letter of Peter proclaims: "Be sober, be vigilant, for the devil, as a roaring lion, walks about, seeking whom to devour."[23] We are called to be awake and aware—seekers of good.

Darkness

As we've seen, Psalm 90 (91)[24] was one of the earliest biblical texts to be associated with prayer at nightfall in both Jewish and Christian traditions. Its verses speak of our putting complete faith and trust in the Divine Presence, who is "bound in love" to us (Listen: example 3). The following verses speak especially of the dangers that come in the darkness:

> You shall not be afraid of any terror by night,
>   nor of the arrow that flies by day;
>
> Of the plague that stalks in the darkness,
>   nor of the sickness that lays waste at mid-day.[25]

What thoughts or feelings do these words evoke for you? I think of "terror by night" as a surprise injury from an external foe, or when I suddenly find myself unprepared for a major challenge. The images of "the arrow that flies" and "the sickness that lays waste at mid-day" remind me of friends cut down in the prime of life during the war in Vietnam and the HIV/AIDS epidemic during the 1980s.

The words of the psalm also remind me of darkness within—ignorance, evil, or sin. We must "be sober, be vigilant," against the "devil, as a roaring lion"—or against the Compline hymn's "nightly fears and fantasies." Our vigilance should be directed especially against ignorance, which may indeed be the real nature of evil. Wayne Teasdale writes that the "philosophies of the East reject the notion of ontological evil"; instead people commit evil actions because "they see some good in it for themselves." Their choices are "saturated by their own ignorance: of the nature of the good itself, of the necessity not to harm others, and of how their actions ultimately harm not only their enemies but themselves."[26]

Consider this parable from Matthew's Gospel:

> Then the kingdom of heaven will be like this. Ten bridesmaids took their lamps and went to meet the bridegroom. Five of them were foolish, and five were wise. When the foolish took their lamps, they took no oil with them; but the wise took flasks of oil with their lamps. As the bridegroom was delayed, all of them became drowsy and slept. But at midnight there was a shout, "Look! Here is the bridegroom! Come out to meet him." Then all those bridesmaids got up and trimmed their lamps. The foolish said to the wise, "Give us some of your oil, for our lamps are going out." But the wise replied, "No! There will not be enough for you and for us; you had better go to the dealers and buy some for yourselves." And while they went to buy it, the bridegroom came, and those who were ready went with him into the wedding banquet; and the door was shut. Later the other bridesmaids came also, saying, "Lord, lord, open to us." But he replied, "Truly I tell you, I do not know you." Keep awake therefore, for you know neither the day nor the hour. (Matt. 25:1–13)

Vigilance is a state of awareness, of being awake to the present moment and the possibilities for good or ill that it presents.

Repentance

In spite of our intentions to do what is good, we are imperfect. Through inattention or ignorance we fail to know or do the right thing. As the apostle Paul puts it, "For I do not do what I want, but I do the very thing I hate. . . . I can will what is right, but I cannot do it."[27] As night falls, it is appropriate to review the events of the day; examine our thoughts, words, and actions; and ask for forgiveness and the time to make changes. A verse of Psalm 4, one of the psalms appointed for Compline as well as part of the Bedtime Shema, may contain the origin of the office itself: "Tremble, then, and do not sin; speak to your heart in silence upon your bed."[28] In most orders of Compline, a confession of sin is included. It provides an opportunity for this reflection to take place.

Our music at Compline often includes texts about repentance at the close of the day. Sometimes we sing a simple prayer (Listen: example 4) that sums up a desire to enter into the silence and reverence of the rest to come, forgiven and renewed:

> Dear Lord and Father of mankind,
> Forgive our foolish ways!
> Reclothe us in our rightful mind,
> In purer lives thy service find,
> In deeper rev'rence, praise.

Drop thy still dews of quietness,
Till all our strivings cease:
Take from our souls the strain and stress,
And let our ordered lives confess
The beauty of thy peace.[29]

As I ask forgiveness, I am reminded of another parable of
Jesus, this one about having a humble heart:

> Two men went up to the temple to pray, one a
> Pharisee and the other a tax collector. The Pharisee,
> standing by himself, was praying thus, "God, I thank
> you that I am not like other people: thieves, rogues,
> adulterers, or even like this tax collector. I fast twice
> a week; I give a tenth of all my income." But the tax
> collector, standing far off, would not even look up to
> heaven, but was beating his breast and saying, "God,
> be merciful to me, a sinner!" I tell you, this man went
> down to his home justified rather than the other; for
> all who exalt themselves will be humbled, but all who
> humble themselves will be exalted. (Lk. 10:8–14)

Jesus showed us by his teachings and his very act of sacrifice
a resolution for our sinful state. This is wonderfully expressed
in a seventeenth-century text that was set to music for the
Compline Choir by its founder, Peter Hallock (Listen: example
5). The first stanza likens our minds to a house with many
rooms, in which the room with memories of our misdeeds
cannot be shut away from the room of our consciousness:

If we could shut the gate against our thoughts
And keep out sorrow from within:
Or memory could cancel all misdeeds,
And we unthink our sin,
How free, how clear, how clean our hearts would lie,
Discharged of such grievous company.[30]

It is only through meditation on Jesus's example and through repentance that we might truly become free.

O Saviour, who our refuge art,
Let thy mercies stand twixt them and us,
And be the wall to separate our hearts,
so that we at length repose us free:
that peace, and joy, and rest may be within,
And we remain divided from our sin.[31]

✳ ✳ ✳

Divine Light

One of my encounters with light and darkness came during a visit I made to New Haven, Connecticut, to hear Compline at Christ Church, near the campus of Yale University. The service, which has been offered there since 2001 and was inspired by the Seattle Compline experience, was nevertheless unique, with a professional choir of men and women in a beautiful church lit only by a hundred votive candles, and with incense rising in front of the altar.

It was a rainy night in April, the last Compline of the season, which at Yale is only observed during the school year. It was storming hard, and the choir took candles with them up to a gallery in one of the transepts (where they were hidden from view) in case the tiny electric lights on their music stands went out during the storm. I sat in the church with perhaps a hundred others, mostly students. It was silent except for the squelch of boots, and a distant cascade of bells from the tower.

A single male voice intoned the beginning. Then the choir sang Psalm 91 in simple plainsong. Suddenly the first lightning struck, briefly illuminating the stained glass images, which burned into my mind as the choir continued. "Thou shalt not be afraid . . . [thunder] . . . of any terror by night." All my thoughts about Compline as a preparation for the terrors of the night, and a revelation of the light that is our safekeeping, came together in those moments. I was confronted as well with the awesome energy of the lightning as it illuminated the images in the windows, and thought of prophets and saints filled with awe as they encountered the Divine Presence.

Images of light indicating God's presence abound in the Bible: the burning bush seen by Moses, the pillar of fire leading the Israelites into the Promised Land, the dazzling light that transfigured Jesus, the "shining garments" of the two angels described by St. Luke in his account of Jesus's resurrection. In Psalm 103(104):2, the divine is described as wrapped "with light as with a cloak"; the modern understanding that light and all created matter is made from the same cosmic material gives an even deeper sense of wonder. And light, in its most powerful manifestations, provokes a reaction of awe, a terrible but holy fear, as I felt in the church at New Haven.

In the midst of Compline is a wonderful text about light from the second chapter of the Gospel of Luke, known as the "Song of Simeon."[32] It's also called the *Nunc dimittis*, after its first line: "Now let your servant depart in peace" (Listen: example 6). Its association with Compline is twofold: it has to do both with experiencing divine light and accepting our mortality in peace (more about the latter in the next chapter).

In the story from Luke, Simeon is an old man who has been told by the Holy Spirit that he will not see death until he has seen the Messiah, God's "Chosen One." He is present in the temple when the baby Jesus is brought there to be blessed in the purification rite, which was required forty days after the birth of a child. Simeon takes the child in his arms and says:

> Lord, now you let your servant go in peace;
> your word has been fulfilled.
> My own eyes have seen the salvation
> which you have prepared in the sight of every people:
> A light to reveal you to the nations
> and the glory of your people Israel.[33]

Simeon, however, is not alone in his revelation; Luke goes on to tell us:

> There was also a prophet, Anna the daughter of Phanuel, of the tribe of Asher. She was of a great age,

having lived with her husband seven years after her marriage, then as a widow to the age of eighty-four. She never left the temple but worshiped there with fasting and prayer night and day. At that moment she came, and began to praise God and to speak about the child to all who were looking for the redemption of Jerusalem.[34]

The theologian Harvey Cox points out that the story of Simeon and Anna is the perfect example of a Midrash, a rabbinical amplification of previous Scripture to make a point.[35] Cox likens this to a jazz riff, where a previous melody is transformed into a new variation. Luke riffs on several passages from Isaiah to refer to the infant Messiah, including 49:6: "I will give you as a light to the nations, that my salvation may reach to the end of the earth."

The reason why this story is forever linked with Compline is that, having been shown the light of Christ, we can now face the darkness, whether it is the coming night or the shadow of death. The birth of Christ was symbolically set by the early church at the time when the northern hemisphere was at its darkest—the winter solstice, when the promise of light was most needed. The Feast of the Purification is celebrated on February 2, the "fortieth day of Christmas," and the *Nunc dimittis* is sung in a procession with many candles. The older English name for the celebration survives as "Candlemas."

Enlightenment and Transformation

We have focused on the qualities of darkness and light separately, but the reality is that both are inextricably part of our spiritual journey. As we walk that path, we see darkness and light as mysteries, not to be solved, but to be accepted as the fabric of life itself. Our goal, should we choose it, is to seek greater enlightenment and communion with the divine. There are many stories of hope—stories that tell us if we seek with earnestness and fervor, we shall find that communion. Here is one example, again from the Gospel of Luke:

> As [Jesus] approached Jericho, a blind man was sitting by the roadside begging. When he heard a crowd going by, he asked what was happening. They told him, "Jesus of Nazareth is passing by." Then he shouted, "Jesus, Son of David, have mercy on me!" Those who were in front sternly ordered him to be quiet; but he shouted even more loudly, "Son of David, have mercy on me!" Jesus stood still and ordered the man to be brought to him; and when he came near, he asked him "What do you want me to do for you?" He said, "Lord, let me see again." Jesus said to him, "Receive your sight; your faith has saved you." Immediately he regained his sight and followed him, glorifying God; and all the people, when they saw it, praised God. (Lk. 18:35–43)

This story is instructive for our own search for enlightenment. The beggar wanted to see so badly that he overcame the voices around him trying to restrain him; in the same way we have to overcome our inner voices that tell us our quest is futile and worthless. The blind man's faith and persistence are a lesson for us, and, with divine assistance, we can also gain our sight.

In addition to confronting inner voices that get in the way, we must address those attachments, evil desires, ignorance within, and the ego that is the "false self" in our search for enlightenment. Sometimes there has to be a major crisis, usually but not necessarily at midlife, a "dark night of the soul" that must be endured before real transformation can occur. As Thomas Merton puts it: "There must be a time when the efforts to live a false life become impeded and blocked, humiliated."[36]

✳ ✳ ✳

One of my times of greatest despair coincided with another visit to Solesmes Monastery in May of 1999. I was alone, making a two-day retreat during the Feast of the Ascension. I awoke in the early hours of the morning, full of tears and grief about a relationship that had been very important to me, that was now ending. I turned on my bedside light, and read these words from Jungian psychologist Robert Johnson: "It is a compliment of the highest order when a man finds that he cannot go farther and that his life is an irredeemable tragedy. His ego consciousness is stalemated, and this stalemate is the only medicine that will drive him out of the Hamlet tragedy and inspire him into a new consciousness.[37] *Johnson was writing about three stages of consciousness—simple, complex, and enlightened— symbolized by the figures of Don Quixote, Hamlet, and Faust. In Faust's case, instead of ending his life by taking poison, he is stopped by hearing a choir singing Easter music. In my case I was roused by the bell at five in the morning to hear Matins, and was soothed by the quiet recitation of the psalms by men who, like me, were seeking their true selves.*

On the road to enlightenment comes a new understanding: that darkness and light are equal aspects of the Divine Presence. The words of the psalmist now assumed a greater meaning for me: "Darkness is not dark to You; the darkness is as bright as the day. Darkness and light to You are both alike."[38] We ultimately perceive the mystery that lies behind the opposites of darkness and light—that if God is truly all in all, then both darkness and light are contained together within the Divine Presence. There can be no resurrection without crucifixion, no life without ego-death, no enlightenment without a dark night of the soul.

FOR FURTHER READING

Johnson, Robert. *Transformation: Understanding Three Levels of Masculine Consciousness.* New York, HarperCollins, 1991.

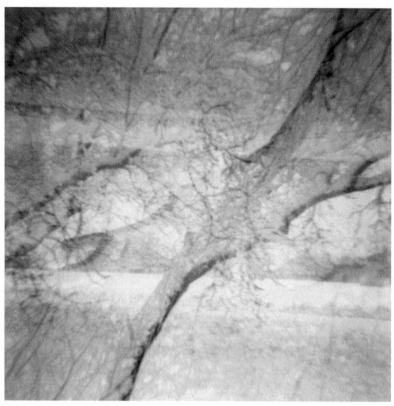

Winter Branches, Madison, Wisconsin   Gabrielle Fine, 2010

5

A Quiet Night and
a Perfect End

DEATH AND LIFE

The Lord Almighty grant us a quiet night and a perfect end.

—ORDER OF COMPLINE[39]

* * *

The words at the beginning of Compline always remind me that our prayers are not only for a peaceful night but also, at the last, a good death. As I prepare for sleep, that "little death," I meditate on the fact that my whole life's journey, every waking and sleeping moment, is a prelude to that moment of transition into what might lie beyond. In that spirit of vigilance as night approaches, I am reminded that death is a great unknown, both in that we know not when and how it will come, or what comes after.

* * *

During the summer of 1965, between my first and second years of college, I took a job as a hospital "orderly," as it was known in those days. After singing Compline on Sunday evenings I did not sleep, but hurried off to work the eleven-to-seven shift at a hospital in Tacoma, about thirty miles away. The job entailed many duties now done by nurses, such as setting up traction, moving patients, and replenishing large oxygen tanks. But the job I most remember was taking bodies to the hospital morgue, where they would lie until someone from a local mortuary would come to retrieve them.

I was most impressed with how mysterious the transition seemed between death and life—the body I held, wrapped in a shroud, still not even very cold—how could this body only an hour before have been alive like me? I carefully put the corpse in a sling to winch it over onto the morgue slab. I lifted up the head almost as if the person were still alive and would not have wanted to be uncomfortable. It was truly difficult, in the physical presence of someone who had recently died, to know that the invisible line between life and death had really been crossed—a line that I too would cross some day. I wondered about that spirit that made me alive, that I felt so vividly when singing—and what would become of it when I died.

Over that summer I also had many experiences with those going through the dying process; the one I remember most was taking care of a beloved piano professor. Whenever I brought something to his room, he always had a smile and a kind word for me. I remember his gentle manner, talking in the hallways of the music building with other students, as well as his confident performances as an accompanist and soloist. That confident, gentle demeanor was evident during his last days, as he struggled with cancer. Toward the end of the summer the day finally came when I got the call to come to his room and take his body, just like the others, to its temporary resting place in the morgue. I tried to emulate his gentleness years later, when I found myself confined to a hospital bed for a long time.

In her lovely book on caring for the dying, Christine Longaker writes of the importance of spiritual preparation for death. A practice "so deeply ingrained that it becomes part of our flesh and bones" can help us to bear suffering during the dying process, as well as give the moment of death itself a good outcome. Although she writes from a Buddhist perspective, her insights are applicable to those of any spiritual outlook. Aside from the efficacy of facing death with hope, such practices can orient and center us as we live through the time we are allotted. Practices like meditation and prayer can also enable us to be with others as they go through the dying process—Longaker writes of the help and peace they can bring even to someone who may have no particular belief or practice.[40]

Two parts of the Compline service have always given me a particular sense of calm and acceptance in the face of the inevitable end of life. The first is a short set of verses and responses between soloist and choir that follows the short reading of Scripture in our singing of the office:

Verse:　Into your hands, O Lord, I commend my spirit;

Resp.:　Into your hands, O Lord, I commend my spirit;

℣.　For you have redeemed me, O Lord, God of truth;

℟.　I commend my spirit.

℣.　Glory be to the Father, and to the Son, and to the Holy Spirit;

℟.　Into your hands, O Lord, I commend my spirit.

The text, known by its Latin name *In manus tuas*, comes from several verses of Psalm 30 (31) ("In you, O Lord, have I taken refuge"), which itself is sometimes included as a fourth Compline psalm. I find this short response to be a litany of assurance and communion in God's presence. We entrust our souls into God's keeping, into that love that permeates all being, the love that brings us to life from the elements of which the whole universe is formed, and when we die transforms us back into that same dust and spirit. When we hear the words, "Into thy hands, O Lord, I commend my spirit," we also know these as some of the last words of Jesus as he hung on the cross, recorded in the Gospel of Luke. For the Christian, the use of this psalm verse reminds us of the offering Jesus made of his life for our salvation. This is a powerful mantra for the Christian, particularly the second half ("for you have redeemed me")—unsaid by Jesus, but implied by his act of love.

A second chant from Compline that informs my attitude toward death is the *Nunc dimittis*, which I have mentioned earlier. Two elderly figures, the priest Simeon and the widow Anna, are the main actors in the story. Simeon vows he will not die until he beholds the Messiah, the one who will fulfill the prophecies to redeem Israel (Listen: example 7). The eighty-four-year-old Anna, a widow for perhaps six decades, worships night and day in the temple. Both recognize in the infant Jesus the long-expected Redeemer, and Simeon, his hopes fulfilled, exclaims that he can now "lie down in peace." As Luke relates the story, I am impressed with the inclusiveness of the message, given by both male and female elders—a song of hope, of deliverance for all peoples, not one people, for the humble widow as well as the venerable priest. And the message of deliverance, from the lips of those confronting their own immanent death, is transformed into much more than the coming of the Messiah; through Jesus's resurrection, Simeon's pronouncement becomes our song of redemption from death itself.

Victimae Paschali *and Eternal Life*

The repetition of chants such as *In manus tuas* and *Nunc dimittis* offer trust and hope in the face of our death. Over the course of a liturgical year of singing a Divine office, many other hymns, prayers, and anthems evoke similar feelings— but I would like to give special recognition to a chant that we sing only once during the year: *Victimae paschali laudes*. This chant, written in the eleventh century, is a *prose* or *sequence* for Easter Day. Hundreds of similar compositions were written during the Middle Ages, but this is one of only a few used today in liturgies of the Roman Catholic Church.[41] We often sing it as the hymn at Compline on Easter Day (Listen: example 8).

The words of this chant move me as perhaps no other—I wait all year to sing it. It is nothing short of the essential message of the Gospels, and hence its place of honor just before the reading of the Gospel on Easter Day, the most important Christian celebration.[42] And it brings us into a resolution of the conflict between life and death.

Victimae paschali laudes Immolent Christiani.	Christians, to the Paschal Victim, Offer your thankful praises.
Agnus redemit oves: Christus innocens patri Reconciliavit peccatores.	A Lamb the sheep redeemeth. Christ, who only is sinless, reconcileth sinners to the Father.
Mors et vita duello conflixere mirando: Dux vitae mortuus, regnat vivus.	Death and life have contended in that combat stupendous; the Prince of life who died, reigns immortal.[43]

This is the story of highest drama: we are born, set on a course that we call *life*, a course that has a common destination in our death. In the medieval poem, life and death are likened to champions competing for our souls, as in the version from the *English Hymnal* that we sing: "death and life have contended in that combat stupendous." In our own times, we might see this as a struggle of two competing ideologies—the idea of death as a complete end to life versus an intermediate stage to something else. These seemingly contradictory states are reconciled by Jesus, through his resurrection.

The event of Christ's resurrection is indeed the central defining aspect of the Christian faith. Even the most cautious scholars have to admit that something happened immediately after the death of Jesus. It transformed the disciples, who had abandoned their leader, into ardent believers who suffered torture and death in Jesus's name and who instituted a new holy day to commemorate the Resurrection. The four Gospels—Matthew, Mark, Luke, and John—written about thirty-five to sixty years after the events of AD 30, were based on earlier unwritten accounts of eyewitnesses, many of whom were living at the time of the writing. The death of Jesus, the empty tomb, the appearances to the disciples, the conversion of the anti-Christian Paul—these and other events point to the truth of the resurrection event.[44]

We live today in an exciting time, when evidence of after-death phenomena similar to the Christian concept of resurrection comes from other spiritual traditions. In 1998, in the province of Kham in eastern Tibet, a Buddhist monk, a "hidden master" named Khenpo A-chos, died, and over the course of seven days his body gradually shrank until nothing remained. Other signs of the "Rainbow Body" tradition accompanied this event: multicolored light, apparitions, mysterious music, and perfume-like scents. In other reported cases, shrinkage of the body occurred, or just hair and nails remained; the 1998 case is not an isolated occurrence.[45] Such effects of intense spiritual practice are also manifest in some Christian saints whose bodies are "incorruptible," and do not decompose. Such human manifestations serve not only to substantiate after-death phenomena but also to give more credence to the resurrection of Jesus as an event of supreme importance.

In all three chants I have mentioned from Compline, the focus is on Jesus—his redemptive act on the cross, his revelation of light and eternal life to all peoples, and his resurrection. Through his teachings and examples we experience the nature of eternal life and come to a right attitude about our death. Jesus said, "I came so that they might have life and have it more abundantly" (Jn. 10:10). Mysteriously, the more we seek our eternal selves, our true selves, the less we fear death. As we empty ourselves, shed the "tent of clay" that is our bodies, our egos, our senses, our thoughts, we fill ourselves with the presence that creates and sustains all. Words fail at this point to describe this relationship to the divine, but perhaps these quotes from the seventeenth-century English mystic poet Thomas Traherne may suffice: "You never enjoy the world aright, till the sea itself floweth in your veins, till you are clothed with the heavens, and crowned with the stars. . . . Till you can sing and rejoice and delight in God, as misers do in gold. . . . Till your spirit filleth the whole world, and the stars are your jewels."[46] It is necessary for us to shed the confining shell of belief, abandoning it for the world of faith, where we are "lost in wonder, love, and praise."[47] A belief—whether it be a naive image of heaven "up there" somewhere, or a science-fed atheism that we're here by chance and become nothing when we die—pales when we enter, in this present moment, into full communion with divine reality. The following words of Alan Watts, with which he concludes *The Wisdom of Insecurity*, are appropriate here. Read them as a summation of his thoughts, then again as a description of death itself:

> The split between I and me, man and the world, the ideal and the real, comes to an end. *Paranoia*, the mind beside itself, becomes *metanoia*, the mind with itself and so free from itself. Free from clutching at themselves the hands can handle; free from looking after themselves the eyes can see; free from trying to understand itself thought can think. In such feeling, seeing, and thinking life requires no future to complete itself nor explanation to justify itself. In this moment it is finished.[48]

On the Threshold

I would like to tell about several experiences, both involving Compline, and both taking me back to that liminal place, that transition point, between life and death.

✳ ✳ ✳

In the final several years of my mother's life, she suffered from increasing dementia. The symptoms of the disease, which include the forgetting of memories, also include the gradual forgetting of bodily functioning, and the last thing to cease for her was the ability to swallow. Other problems precluded the use of a stomach tube, and as her only child I made the decision to put her in hospice care. By this time she had lost all abilities to respond or converse. The attendants at her adult family home and I would spend hours trying to get a few spoonfuls of liquid down the right pipe, but after a while, even that proved futile.

I sat with her in those last few weeks, telling her things that I hoped she could hear, praying, or just being present. As I was praying one evening, I happened to think of reciting Compline, something that came easily to me after decades of singing the office. It was only then that I became truly aware of some of the prayers' relevance to the dying process:

Mother, may the Lord grant you

a quiet night and a perfect end.

Mother, you rocked me, and sang lullabies to me—

I lie down in peace—at once I fall asleep. For you Lord, make me dwell in safety.

Mother, you've lived a wonderful life, and now you can rest from your labors—

Come unto me, all you that labor and are heavy laden, and I will give you rest.

Mother, you've been a model to me in your faith—

Into your hands I commend my spirit. For you have redeemed us, O God of truth.

Mother, be now with God, who knows the number of the hairs on your head, and loves you as uniquely as the print of your iris—

Keep me as the apple of an eye. Hide me under the shadow of your wings.

Mother, help us as we keep watch—

Guide us, O Lord, while waking, and guard us while sleeping. That awake we may watch with Christ, and asleep we may rest in peace.

Mother, now you can go in peace—

Lord, now let your servant depart in peace, for my eyes have seen your salvation.

I don't know if she heard me, but I do know that I became much more aware that night of how much strength my own spiritual practice had given me.

In 2000, the Compline Choir made a trip to England; it wasn't an ordinary choir tour, but rather a pilgrimage to celebrate the fiftieth anniversary since our founder and director, Peter Hallock, had been a student in Canterbury at the Royal School of Church Music. It was in the crypt of Canterbury Cathedral that Hallock and his fellow students would sing Compline, mainly for the benefit of hearing the chants resonate in the wonderful subterranean space.

When we visited Canterbury Cathedral we sang our office of Compline in the choir stalls of the cathedral for the general public. As the service progressed, I recalled that Canterbury was founded by monks, and that Compline would have been sung every evening in this place, with the same chants, over nine hundred years before. It seemed as though the same spirit passed from those ancient voices to the students in 1950, and through Peter Hallock to us, and on to many choirs throughout North America.

Having completed Compline, we had arranged in advance to process down to the crypt, where we would sing, just for our own group, one of Peter's anthems. I was reminded of the medieval custom to process to another chapel after Compline to sing a special anthem, and felt again a connection to those who had gone before. We walked silently past the altar, marking the spot where Thomas Becket had been murdered in 1170, then downstairs to the crypt. We gathered in the middle of the chamber, under the low stone arches, in the final resting place of many of the saints. I thought of the columbarium in the crypt of St. Mark's in Seattle, where the remains of friends and acquaintances lie. We had arrived at our pilgrimage destination.

The anthem Peter had selected was a composition he had written nine years before, using the words of a prayer fashioned from the ending of a sermon given by John Donne: "Bring us, O Lord God, at our last awakening, into the house and gate of heaven." This poem and the occasion of our singing in the crypt at Canterbury has always been linked together for me as a meditation on our dying (Listen: example 9):

> Bring us, O Lord God, at our last awakening
> Into the house and gate of heaven.
> To enter that gate and dwell in that house,
> Where there shall be no darkness nor dazzling, but one
>   equal light;
> No noise nor silence, but one equal music;
> No fears nor hopes, but one equal possession;
> No ends nor beginnings, but one equal eternity;
> In the habitation of thy glory and dominion,
> World without end, Amen.

It was only years later, in writing this book, that I sought out Donne's sermon[49] and discovered how much it says about life and death.

The sermon that Donne preached that day was on Acts 7:60: "And when he had said this, he fell asleep." Lent had just begun, and Donne began his sermon by saying "He that will dy with Christ upon Good-Friday, must hear his own bell toll all Lent."[50] The verse from Acts comes at the end of the life of Stephen, the first Christian martyr, whose last words, as he was stoned to death, were "Lord, do not hold this sin against them," and then, having uttered these words, he died, or—in the King James Version—"he fell asleep." Donne seizes on this short verse of Acts to make two points: first, that we must be something, answer some calling in our lives, and live out our days following the example of a person of integrity, such as Stephen; and second, that having done our best, we will not die, but sleep the sleep of Stephen, a blessed rest until the Resurrection.

We began by thinking of sleep as a little death, and we end by a vision of death as but a sleep. As darkness is succeeded by light, so sleep is followed by waking. Donne concludes his sermon as follows:

> They shall awake as *Jacob* did, and say as *Jacob* said, *Surely the Lord is in this place, and this is no other but the house of God, and the gate of heaven,* And into that gate they shall enter, and in that house they shall dwell, where there shall be no Cloud nor Sun, no

darkenesse nor dazling, but one equall light, no
noyse nor silence, but one equall musick, no fears nor
hopes, but one equal possession, no foes nor friends,
but one equall communion and Identity, no ends nor
beginnings, but one equall eternity. Keepe us Lord
so awake in the duties of our Callings, that we may
thus sleepe in thy Peace, and wake in thy glory, and
change that infallibility which thou affordest us here,
to an Actuall and undeterminable possession of that
Kingdome which thy Sonne our Saviour Christ Jesus
hath purchased for us, with the inestimable price of
his incorruptible Blood. *Amen.*[51]

May we experience eternity now, in this life, a foretaste of
that "one equal music" and "one equal possession," when we
awake from the great sleep.

FOR FURTHER READING

Hamilton, Lisa B. *Daily Prayer for Times of Grief.* Brewster, MA:
Paraclete Press, 2001.

Longaker, Christine. *Facing Death and Finding Hope: A Guide
to the Emotional and Spiritual Care of the Dying.* New York:
Doubleday, 1997.

6

Before the Ending of the Day

CHRISTIAN ORIGINS OF COMPLINE

Before the ending of the day,
Creator of the world we pray,
That with thy wonted favour, thou
Wouldst be our guard and keeper now.

—COMPLINE HYMN
Te lucis ante terminum[52]

* * *

In the summer of 1976, I resigned from a job teaching elementary school music in British Columbia and flew to Scotland to help some friends who had just purchased a North Sea fishing trawler. They needed to get the seventy-foot vessel back to Canada, and I agreed to be a crew member for part of the trip.

We began the journey around the first of October, and by mid-month we were moored on the Isle of Jura, one of the Inner Hebrides on the west coast of Scotland, waiting for a storm to clear. When the weather improved, I decided to go out and do some exploring. The only road led upward, and I climbed for about half an hour until I reached

the crest of a hill. I hopped over a wooden fence and entered an open
pasture where my only companions were a couple of black-faced sheep.
The vista before me was stunning. To the south, across thirty miles
of ocean, was the coast of Ireland; to the west, the hills of Islay, and
beyond them the pale Atlantic, stretching all the way to New York.
Somewhere to the northwest were the Isles of Mull and little Iona, a
great center of monastic life after its founding by St. Columba in the
middle of the sixth century.

I wondered what it was like to look down from those hills to see
the ships coming, bringing monks and supplies bound for Iona. I
wondered how it was to sing with those monks at the end of the day in
that land of rugged coasts, harsh life, and fear of the invader. What
would it have been like to chant Compline with them?

Fifty days after the feast of the Passover in Jerusalem,
the disciples of Jesus of Nazareth, filled with the fire of
the Holy Spirit, brought forth a new faith, rooted in Jewish
tradition but preaching a savior and teacher who rose from
the grave and became present to them in the Eucharistic
feast. By the time of their freedom from persecution by
the Roman Empire in the early fourth century, Christians
had introduced new ways of observing time: reckoning the
year from the date of the birth of Jesus, and worshiping on
Sunday to memorialize the Resurrection. In addition to the
Eucharist, regular times of fixed-hour prayer were observed;
but Compline, as we know it today—a late-evening service,
said or sung either in common or individually—only made

its appearance at the middle of the fourth century. If we want to understand the origin of Compline, we must look at the evolution of the other daily offices.

In their worship, first-century Christians did not follow Jewish prayer practices literally; they established their own meeting places and special days of observance, and formed their own practices in the breaking of the bread, readings, and prayers. They did, however, follow Jewish practice in praying at fixed times of day, and their readings and prayers contained much from the Tanakh, the Hebrew Bible, which provided the context for and prophecy of Jesus. Their prayer times had as their models either (1) the daily morning and evening sacrifices in the temple at Jerusalem, (2) the four services in the synagogues (morning, noon, afternoon, and evening) on Sabbaths and market days, or (3) worship at home: the twice-daily recitation of the Shema.[53]

There are New Testament accounts of Jesus and the apostles praying at various times during the day or night; many of these took place at the hours known to the Romans as Terce, Sext, and None (about nine in the morning, noon, and three in the afternoon), which also corresponded to the Jewish synagogue times.[54]

It is likely that individual prayer during the early centuries of Christianity followed Jewish practices as well. One of the earliest writings, the *Didache* (late first century), encourages Christians to pray three times a day: morning, noon, and before sleep. This parallels the instruction for devout Jews to pray the *Tefillah*, or "prayers of blessing," at the same three times. The *Didache* also encourages praying the Our Father followed by "For yours is the power and the glory for ages."[55] Before sleep, as we've seen, it is easy to imagine early Christians saying some of the prayers from the Bedtime Shema, including the "prayer for restful sleep" and Psalm 90 (91), followed by the Lord's Prayer.

Prayers before retiring are mentioned infrequently during the second and third centuries, although several writers in both the eastern and western Roman Empire recognized this as an appropriate time for prayer: Clement of Alexandria (ca. 150–ca. 215) and Hippolytus of Rome (in his *Apostolic Tradition* from about 215).[56] Hippolytus, in a section beginning "And, if you are at home . . ." advocates praying at the third, sixth, and ninth hours, and then says, "Pray before your body rests on the bed."[57]

By the end of the third century, Christians often gathered together to pray in both morning and evening. They also kept night vigils on special occasions such as Easter and Christmas, and were directed to pray individually at mid-morning, noon, and in mid-afternoon. The evening office, prayed at sundown, which eventually became known as Vespers, was called *Lucernarium*, a name referring to a ceremony to accompany the lighting of the lamps. As part of the liturgy, special prayers were made to Christ as "light of the world." Cyprian of Carthage (d. 258) writes: "Likewise at sunset and the decline of day we must needs pray again. For since Christ

is the true Sun and true Day, when we pray at the decline
of the world's sun and day and entreat that the light may
again come upon us, we are asking for the advent of Christ,
which will bestow upon us the grace of eternal light."[58] One
of the oldest hymns not taken directly from the Bible is *Phos
Hilaron* ("Hail Gladdening Light"), written at the end of the
third century and sung at the beginning of *Lucernarium*. It
has always been a part of Vespers in the Eastern Orthodox
rite, but was included in 1979 by the Episcopal Church as an
optional canticle for Evening Prayer. We sing it occasionally
at Compline in a modern setting by Kevin Siegfried (Listen:
example 10):

> O gracious Light,
> pure brightness of the everliving Father in heaven,
> O Jesus Christ, holy and blessed!
> Now as we come to the setting of the sun,
> and our eyes behold the vesper light,
> we sing your praises, O God: Father, Son, and Holy Spirit.
> You are worthy at all times to be praised by happy voices,
> O Son of God, O Giver of life,
> and to be glorified through all the worlds.[59]

With an edict in AD 313, the emperor Constantine granted
Christians the right to practice their religion without fear
of persecution. This freedom allowed the church to grow
in numbers, but its new status as a state religion favored
the adoption of models of imperial administration. Those

with more countercultural values and a need for a life given entirely to prayer joined a new movement that was already flourishing: monasticism.

Since the time of Jesus, there had been those who lived lives of simple means, spending their time in prayer apart from others as hermits; emulating Jesus's forty days in the desert, many found a home in Egypt, such as Anthony (252–356). About 323 at Tabenna, in upper Egypt, Pachomius (ca. 292–348) founded groups that were truly communal, with each person living in a separate hut but working, eating, and worshiping in common. By the end of the fourth century the number of these communities (for both men and women) had grown to more than seven thousand and had spread to Palestine, North Africa, and to Asia Minor and Greece.

Particularly in the Egyptian monastic communities, worship consisted in the idea of continuous prayer, which was for the most part done in one's individual cell, although the community met in common at least in the morning and evening. Twelve psalms, along with other prayers, prostrations, and the *Gloria Patri* ("Glory be to the Father . . .") made up what might be called a monastic "office." If an office was said or sung every hour for twelve hours, the whole Psalter could be recited at least once a day. Prayer before sleep was no different from prayer at other hours; it consisted of the next twelve psalms in the daily rotation. This grouping concept was influential on both the Byzantine rite as well as monastic foundations in southern France and Ireland.

St. Basil (ca. 330–379) was inspired by travels in Egypt to start monasteries in his native Cappadocia (today central Turkey). It is in his *Greater Asketikon*, a description of how monks should conduct themselves, that we find the first mention of an additional office after Vespers and before retiring. It was called *apodeipnon*, or prayers said "after supper": "And again, at the beginning of the night we ask that our rest may be without offense and free from phantasies, and at this hour also Psalm 90 [91] must be recited."[60] This impetus to say prayers in common before rest was not confined to Eastern monastics. Alypius, bishop of Tagaste (in modern-day Algeria), who was converted with St. Augustine in 386, and founded the first monastery in northern Africa, mentions in his *Ordo monasterii*: "Let there be said the usual psalms before sleep."[61]

John Cassian (ca. 360–435) is also an important figure in the development of the monastic offices. Born in the region of modern Romania, he traveled to Bethlehem in the 380s, spending three years there before going to Egypt, where he lived in a monastic community near Alexandria for another fifteen years. He traveled to Rome and Antioch, and was asked by Pope Innocent I to found a monastery in Marseilles in 415. He brought the style of prayer he knew from Egypt and Palestine to southern Gaul, but his most lasting contribution is the phrase used at the beginning of every office: *Deus in adjutorium*, from Psalm 69(70):2: "Come to my help, O God; Lord, hurry to my rescue." The monastery he founded became the model for many others in southern Gaul, including Lérins and Arles. But perhaps the most significant influence of these monasteries was on St. Patrick, who studied at several "Gallican" monasteries before going on his famous mission to Ireland in 432.

During the fifth century, Compline began to take its place in the life of monasteries and was finally recorded as a separate office in the West in both the *Rule of the Master* (ca. 500–525) and the *Rule of St. Benedict* (ca. 530–560). Both rules come from the area southwest of Rome, and Benedict may have been influenced by the earlier writing. The two orders of Compline are similar,[62] but Benedict's is slightly more concise.

RULE OF THE MASTER	RULE OF ST. BENEDICT
Three "units" of psalmody (each consists of a psalm, *Gloria Patri*, prostration, and prayer)	Opening verse and Psalms 4, 90 (91), and 133 (134).
Responsory	Hymn
Reading from the Apostles	Lesson
Gospel (the canticle *Nunc dimittis?*)	
Rogus Dei (a litany)	Versicle and Litany
Closing Verse	Blessing and Dismissal

With St. Benedict, we actually have the word *Completorium* used for the first time, and the psalms specified exactly by number: "Compline is limited to three psalms without refrain. After the psalmody comes the hymn for this hour, followed by a reading, a versicle, 'Lord, have mercy,' a blessing and the dismissal."[63] And later he says, "The same psalms—4, 90 and 133—are said each day at Compline."[64] The singing of a hymn was an important part of every office. One of these, *Christe, qui lux es et dies,* was sung at Vespers and Compline in Benedict's time, and ever since (Listen: example 11):

> O Christ, you are both light and day,
> You drive away the shadowed night;
> As daystar you precede the dawn,
> The herald of the light to come.[65]

St. Patrick and others brought monasticism from southern Gaul to Ireland in the mid-fifth century. Irish monks were renowned for their ascetic practices, which included chanting all 150 psalms once or twice daily. This extension of the "continuous prayer" model was carried back to England and the European Continent by Irish missionaries at the end of the sixth century. These included St. Columba's mission to Scotland, where he founded the famous monastery at Iona. At Bobbio, one of the new foundations near Milan, the *Bangor Antiphoner* was found, written in the hand of Irish monks.[66] It is perhaps our best guide to how Compline was prayed in Ireland and southern Gaul.

For Irish monks, there were three night offices, at the beginning and middle of the night, and in the early morning before daybreak. The first of these, *Initium Noctis*, began with a *lucernarium* (ceremony of light), and had twelve psalms, organized in groups of three, with an antiphon sung after every third psalm. There are several prayers for this office preserved in the *Bangor Antiphoner*; here is one example, with its Compline-like sentiment:

> Now that the day has run its course, and night has
> come, let us pray
> to the mercy of God, that our minds filled with
> divine things, we
> may be able to renounce the works of darkness.[67]

At the beginning of the seventh century, there were two main models for praying Compline in the West: the Irish-Gallican "continuous prayer" and the concise, ordered offices of St. Benedict. But, as we shall see, the form envisioned by St. Benedict would, in later centuries, prevail over all other practices in Western Christendom, enhanced and unified by what we now know as Gregorian chant.

FOR FURTHER READING

Bradshaw, Paul F. *Daily Prayer in the Early Church*. New York: Oxford University Press, 1982.

Taft, Robert. *The Liturgy of the Hours in East and West*. Collegeville, MN: Liturgical Press, 1993.

Prayer Candles, St. Mark's Cathedral, Seattle

Gabrielle Fine, 2009

7

Seeking God Seeking Me

COMPLINE AND THE MYSTIC PATH

Then the knowing comes: I can open
To another life that's wide and timeless—
—RAINIER MARIA RILKE,
The Book of Hours[68]

* * *

Every Sunday, just before 9:30 PM, the Compline Choir, dressed in our choir vestments, gathers in an anteroom, observing a few minutes of silence before entering the cathedral. We then process down a side aisle to the same back corner where Compline has been sung for almost sixty years—a location that communicates to those in attendance that they are not simply witnessing a "performance"—rather, they are invited to enter into another perception of time, where they are active participants through their listening and their silence.

Silently we wait for several minutes before we begin, while one of us listens with earphones to hear our service being announced on the live radio broadcast. These are moments of blessing for me—in the

waiting comes an opportunity for quiet, for centering, for bringing
my current feelings to bear on the prayer time about to start. There is
a shift in my consciousness and in my sense of time, from something
measured out into something limitless and free. It is something that I
have come to realize has a name: sacred time.

Compline has provided those who sing, and those who listen, with opportunities to enter into sacred time, and to have their own direct experiences of the divine. My own spiritual journey has been framed by this office of prayer, and my lifelong relationship with God has been formed and nourished by it. Every week I feel touched by the presence of those who come for a half hour of silence—to listen, to meditate, and to connect with the Presence that is both within and among us. This direct way of knowing is not a normal part of the regular communal worship of most Christians, and yet can be the most life-changing, compelling part of the spiritual journey.

Quest for the True Self

The spiritual journey begins at the moment we become self-conscious; it originates in questions like: Who are we? Why are we here? What will happen to us? It is at its heart a quest for meaning, which at first "may be only a restless desire for something more."[69] It may come when we have fastened our desires to things that ultimately do not satisfy, as we yearn for greater happiness. We may discover through encounters with nature, art, or personal joys and sorrows a deep connection to and yearning for the Presence that is within and underlies all existence.

How do we begin a journey to find the One that creates and fills all things yet cannot be contained or held? By the time we begin to wonder, we are already on the journey, and we simply begin where we are. My path was through the Christian faith and, at an early age, through exposure to the Divine Hours through Compline. I believe, however, that all paths have come into existence to lead us to our divine source, and that all of us—of all faiths—journey toward the same center. Rami Shapiro observes that "no labeled person can meet the Unlabeled and the Unlabelable. Each religious tradition must be self-transcending."[70] Our own path must enable us to find our divine source directly, individually—but ultimately in a "heart-to-heart" relationship. We benefit from exemplars, teachers, and spiritual directors, but, in the final analysis, it must be our own experience.

I am convinced that this direct knowing comes from some form of mystic encounter with the divine. The existence of God cannot be proved scientifically—any attempt to unravel a particular mystery increases our knowledge of God but inevitably poses more questions. We begin our search by trying to describe what we seek, while realizing that we are attempting to picture the Indescribable. Wayne Teasdale writes:

The Divine Reality . . . is everywhere, in everything, and radiates from all beings. . . . It also appears in the depths of the self and the unconscious, in dreams, creativity, love, wonder, philosophical reflection, poetic inspiration, in chance meetings, and in all the little joys of life. There is no place we can look or be that we will not find God, if only we recognize what we are seeing.[71]

At some point in the search for the divine reality comes a deep revelation as well as a paradox: that if God pervades all (including ourselves), then our search could be just as well described as God seeking us! This is beautifully expressed in Psalm 138 (139), which is one of my favorites among Peter Hallock's psalm settings for the Compline Choir (Listen: example 12). Here are some excerpts that sum up the importance of this psalm to the spiritual journey.[72]

LORD, you have searched me out and known me; *
    you know my sitting down and my rising up;
    you discern my thoughts from afar.
You trace my journeys and my resting-places *
    and are acquainted with all my ways.
Indeed, there is not a word on my lips, *
    but you, O LORD, know it altogether.
You press upon me behind and before *
    and lay your hand upon me.
Such knowledge is too wonderful for me; *

it is so high that I cannot attain to it.
Where can I go then from your Spirit? *
    where can I flee from your presence?
If I say, "Surely the darkness will cover me, *
    and the light around me turn to night,"
Darkness is not dark to you;
    night is as bright as the day; *
    darkness and light to you are both alike.

As the psalm so beautifully describes, the spiritual journey includes both attraction and aversion.[73]

We are attracted to the Divine Presence through encounters with beauty, a sense of peace, or through memorable feelings of forgiveness or grace. In addition to these in my own spiritual life, the devotional texts from Compline, and the ritual connection to something deep within the human consciousness, began to draw me into an experience of God.

At the same time, we constantly avoid encounters with the Divine, through expressions of our own unworthiness, dwelling on our own fear or despair, or seeking diversions that are transitory. Entering into the spiritual life is a constant process of "letting go" of things that hold us back.

One thing that can free us to change and take action is a reminder of our own impermanence, and the passing away of all material things. Many of the texts we sing at Compline speak of seeking our unchanging Source in the midst of the changing universe, such as the "orison" (sung prayer) "Slowly the rays of daylight fade" (Listen: example 13). A line reminds us of "earthly joys that one by one depart," symbolized by the changing of day into night. We need to let go of everything that will ultimately pass away—as one Zen master says, "Why don't you die now, and enjoy the rest of your life?"[74] This is the meaning that I understand in the last line of the orison—that "trust in things Divine" that only comes when we free ourselves from things that are passing away and direct our attention to things eternal.

At the same time that we are letting go of attachments to transitory things, we are deepening our experiences of God through a continual process called *attunement*:

> We shall never be ourselves until we know we are here to become more and more attuned to something bigger and grander than we are. Nothing less than such attunement will pull out of us that which lies waiting to be completed in us. . . . Attunement occurs when we focus ourselves so that our energy begins to open to the single direction of God. . . . Paradoxically, we find that while the power source, God, is far more than anything we can drum up, it also lives in our depths. The more we are attuned to God, the more we become ourselves.[75]

Because of my musical background, I visualize attunement as adjusting the pitch of my own voice to sync with my colleagues; in spiritual attunement we are resonating with the divine moving in us and revealed to us. This is exactly the same process that Thomas Merton describes as finding our "true selves"; it happens as we let go of the "false self," an aspect of the ego that thinks it exists apart from God. The false self seeks to establish a personal identity through the accumulation of deeds, honors, and things. Merton tells us that even the pursuit of spiritual experience can be a manifestation of the false self, if it is sought like an ultimate holy "trophy" that we can brag about to our friends.[76]

Spiritual attunement may begin with a specific event, like a "born-again" experience, or it may begin consciously with a realization that God has always been seeking us—but no matter how we begin, it is a lifelong process, with personal growth in both the conscious and unconscious realms.[77] Attunement has many aspects, including cultivating discernment, establishing values and precepts, implementing spiritual and physical practices, and living a life of compassion.[78] I realize now that my week-by-week encounter through Compline with both text and music has contributed mightily to this search for the "true self" within me.

We must come to the spiritual journey as an empty vessel, devoid of ego and expectation. Through Compline, we seek out the silence, the "no-thing-ness" of God.

Mystic Experience and Contemplative Practices

Direct knowledge of the divine is a meeting, a communion, in our heart of hearts, with our Creator. For me the *experience* of the divine is more important than theory or just knowing *about* the divine. The nature of the experience is nonverbal (associated with the right side of the brain), generating a feeling of unity with the divine and all creation, evoking feelings of connection and compassion. Paradoxically, we find our true selves in this joining with the divine.

The various elements of the Compline service—silence, darkness, and extraordinary sacred music—all transform the attention from left brain to right brain, active to receptive, time-conscious to eternal, and ego-centered to communal. I would like to mention three specific spiritual practices— all processes of contemplative experience—that have been important to me: listening, chanting, and *lectio divina*.

Listening

In the Old Testament, Elijah stands on a mountain to await God's appearance; after wind, earthquake, and fire, God finally appears as a "sound of sheer silence" (1 Kgs. 19:11–12). It is impossible to enter into a mystical experience without first being silent, being in the present moment, and listening actively. For St. Benedict, this was the most important spiritual practice; he begins his Rule for monks by asking each one to listen carefully to his instructions and to attend to them "with the ear of your heart."[79] In the

Benedictine order, listening is a component of obedience. Christopher Jamison, abbot of Worth, a Benedictine abbey in Sussex, England, points out that the word *obedience* comes from the Latin *oboedire* (*ob* + *audire*), which means "to listen in the direction of" something.[80] Going on a silent retreat, meditating, or simply bringing attention and awareness to the present moment help to develop this skill of listening with discernment.

Chanting

Many people think that chanting, or sacred singing, is a specialized art, best left to choirs. Unfortunately, some have come to this conclusion through an experience of rejection, as children, by some misguided music teacher! Actually chanting is quite accessible, and can be as simple or complex as one desires. All chant begins with the breath, then adds vibration—the most basic chant, taught in many meditation classes, is the "Aum": beginning with a deep breath, then expending it slowly, singing on a single tone, gradually changing the vowel from "Ahhhh" to "Ohhhh," and finishing with an "Mmmm." At the same time, one focuses the mind on the breath and the sound, disengaging the automatic processes—an instant stress reducer.

Besides breath, and vibration (or tone), Cynthia Bourgeault describes two other elements of chant: intentionality and community.[81] Especially when the text encompasses more than a repeated phrase or mantra, as in chanting the Psalms, the attention must be directed to the meaning of the words. And when one sings chant in community, one has to actively listen and adjust to the other voices, lessening the ego and making more room for the "true self" to appear. Chanting can be a rewarding spiritual practice, no matter what the complexity—from the simplest singing of a psalm on a single tone to the elaborate Gregorian chants or polyphony I experience weekly at Compline.

Lectio Divina

The practice of *lectio divina*, which may be defined as "holy or sacred reading," has been part of monastic life for centuries and is widely used individually or in group settings today.[82] Very simply, it involves four aspects of dealing with sacred or spiritual text.

> *lectio*—reading the text, preferably aloud
> *meditatio*—selecting a passage, word, or phrase that calls or beckons
> *oratio*—responding by speaking, praying, or writing
> *contemplatio*—resting in God

In the Benedictine community of which I am an oblate (lay member), we practice *lectio divina* by having the passage read aloud several times, followed by each of us telling what word or phrase particularly resonated with us. After another reading, we tell what images or thoughts our word or phrase evoked. After the last reading, we talk about what meaning the word or phrase has in our particular life situation. We then pray, meditate, or journal alone about what we have learned.

The concept of *lectio divina* has been applied to other forms of engaging the senses, as in *visio divina* (art) or *cinema divina* (film). The examples in this book could be used as a kind of *musica divina* by listening to the music at the same time as reading the text associated with the particular example, and then working with it as *lectio divina* as well as responding to the nonverbal feelings engendered by the music.

The following prayer, from the English *Sarum Primer* (1558), seems especially appropriate for those seeking God (or God seeking us) on the mystic path. We often sing these words (in a setting written for us by one of the members of Compline Choir) at the beginning of Compline (Listen: example 14). It speaks clearly of that communion with God that is at the heart of our spiritual journey.

> God be in my head, and in my understanding;
> God be in mine eyes, and in my looking;
> God be in my mouth, and in my speaking;
> God be in my heart, and in my thinking;
> God be at mine end, and at my departing.

FOR FURTHER READING

Bourgeault, Cynthia. *Chanting the Psalms: A Practical Guide with Instructional CD*. Boston: New Seeds, 2006.

Finley, James. *Merton's Palace of Nowhere: A Search for God Through Awareness of the True Self.* Notre Dame: Ave Maria Press, 1978.

Gorsuch, John P. *An Invitation to the Spiritual Journey.* Mahwah NJ: Paulist, 1990.

Jamison, Christopher. *Finding Sanctuary: Monastic Steps for Everyday Life.* Collegeville, MN: Liturgical Press, 2006.

Shapiro, Rami. *Minyan: The Ten Principles for Living a Life of Integrity.* New York: Crown, 1997.

Wynkoop, Lucy, OSB, and Christine Valters Paintner. *Lectio Divina: Contemplative Awakening and Awareness.* New York, Paulist, 2008.

8

From Canterbury to Constantinople

COMPLINE FROM 600 TO 1600

O Christ, who art the Light and Day,
Thou drivest darksome night away!
We know thee as the Light of Light,
Illuminating mortal sight.

—COMPLINE HYMN
Christe, qui, splendor et dies[83]

* * *

On its pilgrimage to England in 2000, our Compline Choir sang Compline at several of the great cathedrals; but at Norwich Cathedral we sang Evensong—that wonderful Anglican blend of Vespers and Compline. It was August 24—the Feast of St. Bartholomew—which in the Middle Ages was the occasion for a summer fair.

At the end of the service, we were asked to observe a tradition for this special saint's day: to process two by two to the high altar, where we were to be led in special prayers. As coleader, I had a perfect view of our route, past the crossing of the north and south transepts, and around the tomb of Herbert de Losinga, the Norman bishop who founded the cathedral and Benedictine monastery in 1096. I wondered what this might have meant to some of the older Anglo-Saxon monks, who would have lived through the Norman Conquest, thirty years before.

As we reached the altar, my eyes were drawn to the bishop's throne, still in its original elevated position (I counted twelve stairs). As I approached, the throne loomed higher and higher, and I imagined myself as a new priest being ordained by one so literally and figuratively above me. The throne became for me a symbol of the bonds and relationships of medieval society—a backdrop for the flowering of monasticism, the growth of the monarchy, and the ultimate clash between king and church that would lead to the dissolution of monasteries under King Henry VIII.

Compline in the West: The Benedictines

At the time of St. Benedict's death in 547, fourteen monasteries, all in the area east and south of Rome, followed his rule. After the sack of the main monastery at Montecassino by the Lombards in 580, Pope Pelagius II gave the monks a home near the Lateran Basilica in Rome, and their main house remained there for the next 140 years. They were thus close to the center of authority in the Western church, and able to spread their influence and their system of organization into other monastic houses.

This would prove crucial to the nature of the Divine Offices prayed in the West.

A key figure in the spread of the Benedictine order was a man named Gregory, born in 540 to a patrician family in Rome; highly educated, he followed a public career through the chaotic days of barbarian conquests. He became a monk in 574, converted his family estates into monasteries, and served as ambassador to the Byzantine court in Constantinople. When he returned to Rome, he became abbot of the monastery he had founded, and was elected pope in 590.

Pope Gregory I became known as "the Great" for a wide range of accomplishments. He was zealous in missionary work, his most notable project being the sending of Augustine and forty monks to England in 596. Beginning with Canterbury, they founded Benedictine monasteries throughout the kingdom. Gregory was also a prolific writer and administrative architect who would set the course of the church for the next five hundred years—a time when monks played a major role in preserving civilization in a time of chaos. And although Gregory was one among many who contributed to liturgical reform, his fame caused his name to be forever associated with the chant of the church, as "Gregorian chant."

The Rule of St. Benedict during this period emphasized a balance between prayer and work (*ora et labora*). As mentioned in chapter 2, there were seven prayer times, or offices, during the day, and one in the middle of the night. Compline was, and still is, quite simple in Benedictine monasticism, with its three unvaried psalms, a hymn, chapter reading, prayers, and blessing.

During the seventh and eighth centuries, Benedictine influence spread throughout the West, with missions from the monasteries founded by Augustine in England sending their own missionaries back to Gaul and the Germanic lands, much in the same way Irish monks had at the end of the sixth century. Benedictine influence spread throughout Gaul as well, and was championed by a new French dynasty, which strengthened its alliance with a more powerful papacy.

The early ninth century has been named the "Carolingian Renaissance," after the crowning, as new Roman emperor, of Charles the Great ("Charlemagne") of France in 800. There was much activity to establish a new "Roman" unity, resulting in the building of monumental churches, the preservation of classical texts, and the reorganization of churches and monasteries in conformance to papal and Benedictine authority.[84]

Gregorian Chant

The alliance of the papacy with the new imperial power in the West not only forced monasteries to conform to the Rule of Benedict but also standardized the liturgy, conforming it to that of Rome. Cantors from Rome transmitted the music of the chant orally, but notated manuscripts began to appear, first for the Mass, and then for the offices. It is not until the end of the tenth century that we have any notated manuscripts containing Compline, but even then the music was merely notated signs written above the words—still only an aid to memory. With the invention of the musical lined staff in the mid-eleventh century, precise pitch could be indicated, and from that period we have the earliest legible chant melodies, such as the Compline hymn, *Te lucis ante terminum* (Listen: example 15).

From the seventh through the eleventh centuries, all the offices received additions to the core material of Gregory's time. Compline, especially in monastic use, remained quite stable but added a few features, such as an opening reading from 1 Peter ("Be sober, be vigilant"), as well as a general confession of sin. Under the Carolingians, the offices, using liturgies fresh from Rome, were recited in cathedrals (cities still worshiped at one central location until the creation of parishes in the eleventh century). It was in the cathedrals that new elements were added to Compline, such as (1) an antiphon before and after the psalms; (2) the addition of a fourth psalm, 30 (31), with its phrase "Into your hands I commend my spirit"; (3) the short response *Custodi nos domine* ("Keep me as the apple of an eye"); and (4) the canticle *Nunc dimittis* ("Lord, let your servant depart in peace") with its antiphon "Preserve us, O Lord, while waking"). In addition, antiphons and responses began to be varied according to the liturgical season.

Compline in the Byzantine Rite

I want to turn our attention now to the history of Compline as it developed in the traditions of Christianity in the eastern Roman Empire. In this book, where the focus is necessarily on my own heritage, the office in Western Christendom, and in a chapter covering a thousand-year history, a description of Compline in the Eastern rites unfortunately has to be brief, and by no means does justice to what are many living traditions today. Also, I will limit our discussion to just the Byzantine office, omitting many other Eastern liturgies in which Compline is included at various times of the year.[85]

The Byzantine rite, as typically practiced in the Hagia Sophia, the main cathedral of Constantinople, was influenced during the fifth through the eighth centuries primarily by the monastic and cathedral rites practiced in Antioch, and to a lesser extent by those of Alexandria. Another factor was the adoption of the Divine office of Palestine by the Monastery of Studios in Constantinople in 799, and this office coexisted alongside the rite of Hagia Sophia until Constantinople fell to the Crusaders in 1204. After Constantinople was recaptured in 1291, the liturgy was reconstituted on the more monastic lines of Studios, and the chant continued to be revised and expanded until the final fall of Constantinople to the Ottoman Turks in 1453. Further developments took place in the various lands of Eastern Orthodoxy—the Middle East, Greece, Romania, Bulgaria, Serbia and Russia—to build the liturgies that we have today.

Two versions of Compline have evolved in the Eastern Orthodox Church, known as Small and Great Compline. Small Compline is more in keeping with the length of monastic Compline in the West, with just three psalms. When Small Compline is served, it may be read and/or chanted individually or corporately, but Great Compline is always said in common, with some parts chanted by a choir. Great Compline is a penitential office that is served, with some exceptions, on the weeknights of Great Lent and the lesser Lenten seasons, as well as Monday and Tuesday of Holy Week and the eves of Nativity, Theophany, and Annunciation. It is much longer than Small Compline, consisting of three parts, the third of which contains much of the material of the smaller office. Each part of Great Compline begins with psalms and includes the repetition of the *Kyrie eleison* ("Lord, have mercy") forty times, followed by the hymn, "More honorable than the cherubim." Part 1 contains the hymn "God is with us" (Listen: example 16) and the Nicene Creed, and as many as seven psalms, including Psalm 90 (91). Both Great and Small Compline have toward their conclusion prayers of mutual forgiveness, preceded (in Small Compline) by the "O Theotokos," which is similar in sentiment to the "Ave Maria" or Marian Antiphon in the Western church.

Compline in the West: Later Middle Ages

The years 1200–1500 saw the beginning of three important practices in how the Divine Office was practiced in the West:

recitation by individuals in private, proliferation of the Books of Hours for both clergy and laity, and increasing devotion to the Virgin Mary. Each of these had an effect on Compline.

In chapter 50 of his Rule, St. Benedict allows monks who cannot be at the oratory to pray the particular office in their place of work. As early as the eleventh century, the first breviary, a small, portable book containing the prayers for all the offices, was produced.[86] So, although one was required to pray the offices in the oratory when in physical proximity to the rest of the monks (or in the church, for cathedral canons), one could pray individually out of necessity. When dioceses were broken up into parishes in the mid-twelfth century, priests began to pray the offices by themselves as they traveled about their parish. As the number of itinerant friars and students increased during the thirteenth and fourteenth centuries, so did the practice of private prayer.

As early as the eighth century, formal liturgical devotions to the Virgin Mary were composed, but by the tenth century there were complete offices known as "The Little Office of Our Lady." This was a complete cycle of all eight offices, with particular psalms, hymns, readings, and responses appropriate for Mary in each office; the Little Office of Our Lady was commonly prayed on Saturdays.

As breviaries proliferated and the idea of private recitation of the office caught on, "books of hours" began to be created for the laity. These small manuscript prayer books became quite popular, even though some, very lavishly illuminated, were affordable only to the nobility. With the advent of the printing press, these prayer books became much more available to ordinary people. The typical contents were a Calendar, selected Gospel Readings, Prayers, Hours of the Virgin, Hours of the Cross, Hours of the Holy Spirit, the Seven Penitential Psalms, and Office of the Dead. In a given set of hours, Compline consisted of the basics: opening responses, three psalms specific to the theme, a hymn, chapter reading, responses, *Nunc dimittis* with antiphon, a specific prayer, and final responses.[87]

The increased devotion to the Virgin Mary led to the composition of antiphons, some of which began to be used apart from their psalm verses, or as special offerings sung in the "Lady Chapel." In the twelfth through the fifteenth centuries, special offices and private Masses were said as parts of gifts or endowments in return for the granting of indulgences. In addition to these, "votive antiphons" were another way of rendering such a service in return of bequests. It became quite common to sing an antiphon to Mary at the end of Compline, and four such antiphons, composed in the eleventh and twelfth centuries, eventually came into use throughout the liturgical year. In England, for example, the four antiphons were adopted as early as 1254, but ordered in all monasteries by a general chapter of the Benedictines in 1343.[88] In the fifteenth and sixteenth centuries, the votive anthem in England became a high art form in the hands of composers like Thomas Tallis (Listen: example 17).

Here is an example of the parts of Compline from the later Middle Ages, as taken from the Salisbury Antiphonal (Sarum Rite) in England. It shows the basic Benedictine order, augmented to form a typical "cathedral" setting:[89]

OPENING: including *Deus in adjutorium*

PSALMS: 4, 30 (31), 90 (91), 133 (134) with proper antiphon

CHAPTER: *Tu in nobis* ("Thou O Lord art in the midst of us")

HYMN: normally *Te lucis ante terminum* ("Before the ending of the day")

RESPONSE: *Custodi nos* ("Keep us as the apple of an eye")

NUNC DIMITTIS: with antiphon

KYRIE—Christe—Kyrie

OUR FATHER AND AVE MARIA: said privately, then together, "But deliver us from evil"

SHORT VERSICLE AND RESPONSE: *In pace in idipsum* ("We will lay us down in peace")

APOSTLES' CREED: said privately, then together "The resurrection of the body . . ."

RESPONSES: beginning *Benedicamus Patrem* ("Let us bless . . .")

CONFESSION AND ABSOLUTION

RESPONSES: beginning *Deus tu conversus* ("Turn us
again, O Lord")

PRAYER: *Illumina quesumus Domine* ("Lighten our
darkness, O Lord")

CLOSING RESPONSES

VOTIVE ANTIPHON: usually an Antiphon to the
Virgin

Compline in the Reformation and Counter-Reformation

The sixteenth century saw not only the birth of the
Protestant churches but sweeping reforms in the Catholic
Church as well. Of the many revisions of the breviary by
Catholic reformers, two are noteworthy: (1) the editions
by the Spanish cardinal Francisco Quinones in 1535, which
added particular psalms to the weekdays of Compline but left
Sunday Compline with its usual psalms; and (2) the edition
of Pius V of 1570, after the reforms of the Council of Trent
(1545–1563) had been implemented. Quinones's breviary
had been intended for private recitation, but the Pius V
breviary restored the "choral" parts for public recitation.

In the British Isles, the creation of the Church of England
brought widespread change, which affected the chanting
of the offices, both through reform of the liturgy and—
source of greatest chaos—the dissolution of the monasteries.

Between 1536 and 1541, 825 monasteries, priories, convents, and friaries were dissolved or re-formed. In most cases, monasteries were closed, their assets seized, and their buildings left to ruin. But the monastic cathedrals such as Norwich were re-formed as secular cathedrals, with the monks either becoming canons or pensioned off.

The Divine Office was itself changed under Archbishop Thomas Cranmer, who applied Quinones's reforms to the Book of Common Prayer (1549). In particular, the offices were shortened to just two, recited in the morning and evening. Evening Prayer (Evensong) was a combination of Sarum Vespers and Compline, translated into the vernacular; the only elements of Compline that were brought into Evensong were the canticle *Nunc dimittis*, the creed, and one of the collects (prayers). Cranmer also allowed for an anthem to be sung at the end of the service, if a choir was present. I always smile when I hear Evensong and think that it was too hard for Cranmer to let go of the votive antiphon tradition.

At the end of the sixteenth century, Compline in Western Europe was prayed, as a separate office, only in the Roman Catholic Church and, outside of monasteries and large cathedrals, had become a private practice among the clergy and a growing number of the laity.

FOR FURTHER READING

MacCulloch, Diarmaid. *Christianity: The First Three Thousand Years.* New York: Penguin, 2009.

Saulnier, Dom Daniel, OSB, and Mary Berry, CBE, trans. and ed. *Gregorian Chant: A Guide to the History and Liturgy.* Brewster, MA: Paraclete Press, 2009.

Taft, Robert. *The Liturgy of the Hours in East and West.* Collegeville, MN: Liturgical Press, 1993.

Flentrop Organ, St. Mark's Cathedral, Seattle   Gabrielle Fine, 2009

9

To the Supreme Being

BEAUTY

Our unassisted hearts are barren clay
Which of its native self can nothing feed.

—MICHELANGELO BUONARROTI
(1475-1564)[90]

* * *

It has been my good fortune to be a part of a group whose purpose for more than five decades has been to pray a monastic office as well as to provide experiences of great musical beauty. Although singing the Office of Compline weekly is the stated purpose of the Compline Choir, the group has always been a place to explore beauty in sacred music, and partake in an experience that is mystic and transcendent. Similar to any group at prayer, especially monastic communities, it is self-contained, and what motivates the singers to keep coming year after year is their own personal experience and only secondarily the experience they provide for those who attend the service. From its beginning, the Compline Choir has been formed of professional-level singers, never compensated, many of them organists and/or choir directors in other churches, and most from communities other than St. Mark's Cathedral, who come not only to pray the office but also to partake of an aesthetic experience not offered elsewhere.

There is a difference between the Compline Choir and other types of choirs that may not be evident to the casual observer. For instance, the typical Christian church choir's purpose is to assist the assembly at worship as well as inspire through musical offerings or special performances. Or a concert choir may sing sacred music for an audience that has purchased tickets for the privilege of listening. In both cases there is a relationship between choir and "audience" in which the choir needs the assembly as auditors or consumers of their craft. But because the Compline Choir is engaged in a self-contained activity, there is an element of what we do that will always be for me a personal encounter with beauty in which my colleagues and I are the auditors and partakers of the mystical encounter with the divine.

My personal experience of beauty in worship and the relation of beauty to the life of the Spirit in general is the subject of this chapter; it will concern not only meaningful experiences with the beautiful but also how we, as our own "artists," bring the beauty from within to others. I want to begin by drawing some general conclusions about beauty and the search for goodness in all of life's experience, and later talk about a specific musical example from Compline and the weekly inspirational experience of working with Peter Hallock, not only as founder of the Compline Choir but also as composer of many works that give us glimpses of the Divine Presence.

Beauty, Quality, and Taste

Beauty, as described by Thomas Aquinas, is the quality or state of being "that which pleases on being perceived."[91] One may speak of specific aspects that identify something as beautiful; Elaine Scarry, in her short book on beauty, mentions some of them.[92]

- Beauty inspires replication or imitation. A beautiful face, for example, inspires Leonardo da Vinci to make sketch after sketch of the remembered image.
- Beauty is sacred, having an immortal nature, seemingly unprecedented. Even works that have been inspired by others can be traced back to something that is without antecedent.
- Beauty is lifesaving—quickening the heart and welcoming to the soul.

Scarry goes on to point out that in the pursuit of beauty, as in that of truth or justice, there is a relationship between beholder and the object beheld. Pursuers of truth become more knowledgeable, and those pursuing justice become

104 * *Prayer As Night Falls*

more just. Beauty may manifest itself to the beholder in several ways: in the act of replication or bringing new beauty into the world; in the transformation of one's interior life; and in the sense of "aliveness" in the beholder that results in a reciprocal desire to keep alive or preserve the beautiful object.[93]

The above-mentioned characteristics all help to define beauty, but seeking and finding it is a personal matter. We bring our individual qualities of perception, enjoyment, and judgment, which combine to make up "taste,"[94] to choose those things that are more or less aesthetically pleasing to us. The selection of things that are beautiful depends greatly on the context of our current situation, as well as all the personal experiences that have influenced who we are at the time of the choice. This selection is even more important if we realize that we all have many opportunities every day to opt for the beautiful.

As I sing Compline, I am constantly engaged with the "mechanics" of making beauty in music, from the simplest chants to the most complex anthems. I was asked once if I ever got tired of singing the unchanging portions of the chant week after week—I replied that perhaps in my younger days I experienced boredom, but I now look at each time as a new opportunity to sing each passage a little bit better. I was reminded of the central character in the movie *Groundhog Day*, who wakes up every morning having to experience, day after day, exactly the same series of events. After passing through the stages of apathy, anger, and despair, he eventually decides to make each moment better and better, becoming of service to others and perfecting each encounter. This attitude of seeking after "higher quality" is the same as what Robert Pirsig calls "gumption," which he equates with the Greek *enthousiasmos*, "filled with *theos*" (filled with God).[95]

The concepts of beauty, quality, and their place within the spiritual life were solidified for me through a rereading of Pirsig's quasi-autobiographical *Zen and the Art of Motorcycle Maintenance*. As he journeys across the United States with his son on a motorcycle, he recounts a spiritual and metaphysical journey of his own past, in which he searches for and finds the essence of what he calls Quality (with a capital *Q*). Quality is present in that "non-intellectual awareness" that occurs exactly in each present moment. The conceptual awareness comes afterward, and reflects what an object was in the past. Quality is the only reality, the source of all subjects and objects[96]—the essence of being, the source of our perception, synonymous with the divine creative force. What we do in relation to a given perception—our actions—also partakes of Quality, be it high or low. As for art, Pirsig defines it as "high-quality endeavor. . . . Or, if something more high-sounding is demanded: Art is the Godhead as revealed in the works of man."[97]

When we are working in a "high-quality endeavor," we are working with God (or working with Goodness, seeking the Good). This may not be what we normally consider "art"—

but any activity, when it is done with "gumption," with high quality, becomes art, whether it is chanting, motorcycle maintenance, or ordinary household duties. Most crucial to this understanding is that in all creative acts we are engaged in a cooperative endeavor with the divine and are linked to that creative force that underlies all existence. As expressed by Michelangelo in the words that opened this chapter, "our unassisted hearts" are indeed "barren clay," and our work only becomes manifest through divine grace. In order to give anything back to the world, this process has to take place within. Joan Chittister writes: "What we do not nourish within ourselves cannot exist in the world around us because we are its microcosm. . . . To revivify the soul of the world, we ourselves must become beauty. Where we are must be more beautiful because we have been there than it was before our coming."[98] Our Office of Compline is a wonderful blend of a communal worship experience with the thrill of making art, of producing music, which, of all the arts, lives especially in the present moment. Such moments of creative art can often become that very communion with the divine that we seek on our spiritual journey. The question of whether mystic communion comes through prayer or beauty becomes moot; it is through either, or through both—but it is real, and it has been the main motivation for my singing of the office for the major part of my lifetime.

Ecstatic moments remind us, however, of Thomas Merton's warning about the intrusion of the ego into the experience.

Just like any "high-quality" endeavor, the art itself can become one's own religion, or as Paul Tillich defined it, one's "ultimate concern."[99] One has to be especially careful when making art within a sacred context, because the art is created with divine assistance and reveals the divine, but it should not become the object of worship or the ultimate goal of religious experience (as when I hear from another musician "Music is my religion"). Care also has to be taken not to be sidetracked by forms of artistic expression exclusively aimed at making one "feel good" and not leading toward that tension that causes one to think and feel deeply about matters of faith.[100] I suppose that is why the context is so important to the making of sacred music. In our Compline service, which is oriented toward the mystic and meditative, sounds that transport the consciousness from the everyday can actually take us to a sacred space and time apart from the mundane or temporal. Of all these special types of music, chant seems to be perhaps the most effective in this transformative change, because its musical language is used exclusively in a kind of dialogue with the divine.[101]

Sicut Cervus

I wanted to give an example of a piece of music that takes a direct approach to invoking sacred space and time: a composition by the great sixteenth-century master Giovanni Pierluigi da Palestrina (ca. 1525–1594). Like chant, it is an example of sacred music whose impact is transformative, especially in a contemplative service like Compline. Our example is *Sicut cervus desiderat* (Listen: example 18). It is perhaps the best-known and most often performed choral selection from the sixteenth century. Obviously, we have a work whose beauty is undisputed, but I would like to show it in a different light—as an adjunct to mystic contemplation, an aspect not often considered.

Originally the first part of a two-part motet (a free composition of the Renaissance not based on a preexisting Gregorian chant), the text is from Psalm 42:1: "As the deer longs for the water-brooks, so longs my soul for you, O God"—a simple, direct thought, the thirst for enlightenment, for "living water." Palestrina chooses to set the first words to a gentle, rising but undulating line, which perhaps suggests the calm, gentle progression of a deer grazing along the banks of a stream, or the slow steady progression of a soul's journey in faith.

Sic - ut cer - vus de-si - de - rat ad fon - tes a-qua - rum,___

Each of the four vocal parts joins in imitation of the passage, creating a counterpoint of both text and melody, magnifying both as they are woven through time. The harmony produced by the individual voices as they sound simultaneously provides a vertical aspect along with the horizontal movement of each melody. Here are the first few phrases:

Each new phrase of the text is set in this way, with a new melodic idea introduced and sung by each part at a different time. This is the classic Renaissance "imitative" technique. But for me the contemplative part begins when I try to listen to all the voices at once—a tapestry woven from threads of different vocal colors, each telling the same story. I'm especially moved when all parts sing *anima mea* ("so *my soul* longs for Thee, O God"). It is not just "my soul," but each of us, represented in the individual strands, but united in a single idea, a single prayer. As the piece ends, we feel that we've been part of a corporate activity in some sacred "place" apart from our individual consciousnesses.

As a participant, my own experience of such sacred choral music becomes a process akin to meditation. The more I am able to let go and not let myself become distracted, while resting in the meaning of the text, the more it becomes pure contemplation. Of course, the less I have rehearsed the music, the more I must direct my attention to the mechanics of performance, and the less I can achieve the desired state of "flow." But when I know my part, and can let go and hear the other parts around me, then I become lost in not only my own meditation but also in the group effort that is producing the work of art. This is a very special communal experience; to describe it merely as a "musical performance" does not do it justice. Perhaps in listening to the example you can imagine yourself singing one of the parts and begin to feel this communion as well.

Peter Hallock

The whole aesthetic ethos of Compline at St. Mark's owes much, if not all, to the Compline Choir's founder and director, Peter Hallock. Organist and choirmaster at St. Mark's Cathedral for forty years (1951–91) and director of the Compline Choir from 1956 to 2009, his many compositions have added much to the scope and direction of liturgical music in the Episcopal Church over the last six decades. A list of his many innovations and accomplishments, aside from the development of the Compline service, would have to include the following:[102]

- Championing the concept of the neo-Baroque mechanical-action pipe organ, resulting in the installation of a large instrument by D. A. Flentrop in St. Mark's Cathedral in 1965
- Popularizing the art of the "countertenor" voice in North America
- Introducing Flemish handbells into worship and the use of brass instruments for Easter services
- Composing *The Ionian Psalter*, a complete setting of the Psalms for the three-year lectionary cycle of the Episcopal and Lutheran Churches
- Introducing period instruments in Seattle performances of Handel's *Messiah*

All this, plus his interests in unique home design, Japanese gardens, cooking, printing, puppetry, and weaving, will have to wait for another book. His whole ouvre has been an enduring example of *enthousiasmos* for all of us who have known and worked with him.

From the first time I sat down to rehearse with the Compline Choir in October 1964, I realized that I was in a group entirely different from the choirs I had sung with before. For one thing, we would meet typically at eight o'clock on Sunday evening, rehearse the music, and then be singing it on live radio an hour and a half later! Also, there was more of a collegial nature about the group, since many of us were involved in directing our own ensembles outside the group. There was quite a bit of give-and-take as we chose and rehearsed the changeable parts of the service.

Peter's approach to rehearsal was also different. Although he focused on exactness of pitch, diction, blend, and rhythm, Peter was more concerned about things like the rhythmic form of a phrase, *arsis/thesis* (activity/repose), and emotional *and even theological* content—things that really made each piece come alive. And he was not averse to stopping the rehearsal while he made points that most would term "extramusical," but in reality were the very things our singing needed to achieve that higher quality. But most of all, Peter was a constant example of the creative process as a composer in our midst, writing pieces for us that he changed and adjusted during rehearsal, in a kind of personal laboratory. In this way we came to see every piece, even those by composers long dead, as a fresh creation, coming alive in the present moment.

Over the years, I came to realize the source of Peter's unusual approach to rehearsal as well as the quality of his compositions and the spiritual experience inherent in performing them—his innate mysticism. It is not surprising that upon reading Matthew Fox's "Twenty-One Running, Working, Experiential Definitions of Mysticism" in his book *The Coming of the Cosmic Christ*, Peter identified with most of the characteristics of a mystic.[103] Noteworthy among these are

(1) direct experience of the divine rather than secondhand knowledge; (2) right-brain locus (the seat of synthesis, connection-making, and wisdom); (3) a self-critical nature, in which false images of oneself are rejected, as well as the false in religion; (4) a childlike, playful attitude; and (5) the birthing of images, that is, creativity.[104]

The Compline Choir's love for new works has inspired many pieces written by both current and former choir members as well as composers outside the group. Many of the examples in this book are the product of these artists. Here I am reminded of the property of beauty to inspire imitation. The flowering of an artistic community associated with the Compline Choir, and the model it gives to others, is a story echoed throughout history.

Beauty does draw attention like a magnet, and inspires imitation, whether conscious or unconscious. And every beautiful act, every inspired song, draws us closer and closer to our Divine Source. Peter Hallock's setting of "To the Supreme Being," Michangelo's poem quoted at the outset, is all about beauty (Listen: example 19), and makes a fitting summary to what has been said here:

> The prayers we make will then be sweet indeed
> If Thou the spirit give by which we pray.
> Our unassisted hearts are barren clay,
> Which of its native self can nothing feed:
> Of good and pious works Thou art the seed,
> Which quickens only when Thou say'st it may.

Unless Thou show to us Thine own true way—
No one can find it, Lord! Thou must lead.
Do thou, then, breathe those thoughts into our minds
By which such virtue may be bred,
That in thy holy footsteps we may tread.
The fetters of our tongues unbind,
That we may have the grace
By which our songs may rise to Thee
That we may sound thy praises everlastingly.

The composition is illustrative of Peter's sense that what he produces only happens with divine assistance. The words are a reminder to all of us, in all that we create, that "Of good and pious works *Thou* art the seed, / which quickens only when *thou* say'st it may."

FOR FURTHER READING

Brown, Frank Burch. *Good Taste, Bad Taste, and Christian Taste: Aesthetics in Religious Life.* New York: Oxford University Press, 2000.

Fox, Matthew. *The Coming of the Cosmic Christ.* San Francisco: Harper & Row, 1988.

Pirsig, Robert M. *Zen and the Art of Motorcycle Maintenance.* New York: Bantam, 1974.

Scarry, Elaine. *On Beauty and Being Just.* Princeton: Princeton University Press, 1999.

Order of Compline, St. Mark's Cathedral, Seattle Gabrielle Fine, 2009

10

Old Wine in New Bottles

COMPLINE FROM 1600 TO THE PRESENT

In this, most gracious Father, hear,
With Christ, thy equal Son, our pray'r,
Who, with the Holy Ghost and thee;
Doth live and reign eternally. Amen.
—*The Garden of the Soul* (1775)[105]

✳ ✳ ✳

On my first trip to the Abbey of Saint-Pierre de Solesmes in 1987, several members of our group were allowed to see the room where the monks had done their chant research. Our guide, Brother Gregory, put a massive key into the lock of the large oak door, which, like most of the abbey, surely dated from the nineteenth century. I felt for a moment like I was part of a Lewis Carroll story, and wondered whether I would remain the same size if I walked through the door.

We went into a good-sized room with old wooden desks and cabinets. Here the monks had assembled copies of all the surviving manuscripts of medieval chant and compared them to find an "ideal" version of the melodies, which Solesmes had published in the official editions at the beginning of the twentieth century. Their research work was ongoing, especially after Vatican II.

Brother Gregory opened one of the cabinets and showed us a large page where a single section of chant had been copied, line by line, from many different manuscripts. Then the groups of notes could be compared vertically to determine the most typical reading of the melody. It was so exciting to be in the room where this great project had been carried on for decades.

There are two main developments in the history of the Divine Office and Compline in the West from the Reformation to the mid-twentieth century. One took place in Roman Catholicism prior to the Vatican Council of the early 1960s, while the other was the growth of Anglo-Catholic sentiments that eventually resulted in Compline becoming included in the proposed Book of Common Prayer of 1928. It is significant, however, that, among the various offices, the basic shape of Compline in both Catholic and Anglo-Catholic traditions remained fairly stable from 1600 through 1960.

Roman Catholic Compline, 1600–1960

In seventeenth-century France, there were several opposing views among Catholics concerning the offices. One faction liked the simplified Pius V breviary of 1570, but others wanted to preserve parts of the office that pertained to "Gallican" saints and local customs. It was almost fifty years after the Council of Trent before its decrees were finally accepted by the French Assembly of the Clergy in 1615.[106] Also, French scholars worked throughout the century on various improvements to the office, such as allowing for all 150 psalms to be prayed in a given week. The conservative Jansenist movement favored exclusion of all prayers not based on Scripture. These various influences resulted in the publication of the Paris Breviaries of 1680 and 1736.

The growth of the Enlightenment led not only to greater biblical scholarship but also to the antiroyalist and anticlerical movements that contributed to the French Revolution. As part of that revolt, the government suppressed all monasteries in 1789–90. One of these closed monasteries was Saint-Pierre de Solesmes, near the small village of Sablé. A young priest from the area, Prosper Guéranger, learned of the impending demolition of the monastery and undertook to raise the money to save it and reestablish a Benedictine community there in 1833. Solesmes was officially recognized as an abbey by Rome four years later.

Under Guéranger's leadership the monastery prospered, but his greatest achievement was the reform of the liturgy and sacred chant. As a representative of the "ultramontane movement," which advocated for papal authority (especially through the First Vatican Council in 1868), Guéranger worked to replace the French breviaries and return to the purity of the Roman offices. More importantly, he began the work of restoring the Gregorian melodies of the chant, and developed a style-ideal of singing that became the foundation of modern-day chant performance. The monks of Solesmes began to assemble copies of all the major medieval manuscripts of chant, greatly facilitated by the invention of photography. By 1883, Solesmes had published its first book of chants for the Mass.

In the pontificate of Pope Pius X (1903–14), there were several major reforms of both music and liturgy. In his *Motu Proprio, Tra Le Sollecitudini* of November 1903, Pope Pius X imposed strict reforms on all church music, calling Gregorian chant "the supreme model for sacred music," forbidding anything sung in the vernacular or in a theatrical manner, and eliminating, for the most part, all instruments except the organ in sacred liturgies.[107] He also reformed the breviary by 1913, reducing the number of psalms but still allowing for all 150 psalms to be sung in a given week. The monks of Solesmes assisted the process by publishing the official editions of the chants for the Mass (*Graduale Romanum,* 1908) and for the Divine Office (*Antiphonale Romanum,* 1912).

Compline for Sundays in Pius X's breviary only differs slightly from the 1570 breviary of Pius V. Psalm 30 (31) was eliminated, leaving the same three psalms that St. Benedict had suggested almost fourteen hundred years before. For the rest of the weekdays, Pius X appointed other psalms for Compline, in groups of three (which might include just two psalms)—for example, Compline for Mondays had Psalm 6 and two sections of Psalm 7. The most important change in the breviary, however, was that now the typical chant melodies had been researched and restored. The following shows Pius X's order of Compline for Sundays, which, with the exception of the missing Psalm 30 (31), is exactly the same as Pius V's Compline of 1570—a remarkable preservation of the office as well as restoration of the melodies:

INTRODUCTION: *Noctem quietam*
    ("a quiet night and a perfect end")

SHORT LESSON: *Fratres: Sobrii estote*
    ("Brothers, be sober, be vigilant")

LORD'S PRAYER: said silently

CONFESSION AND ABSOLUTION: by priest and choir

BEGINNING SENTENCES: *Converte nos, Deus*
    ("Convert us, O God . . . O God, come to my
    assistance")

ANTIPHON AND PSALMS: 4, 90 (91), and 133 (134)

HYMN: *Te lucis ante terminum*
    ("Before the ending of the day")

CHAPTER READING: *Tu autem in nobis*
    ("You are in the midst of us, O Lord")

SHORT RESPONSES: *In manus tuas, Custodi nos*
    ("Into your hands, O Lord," "Keep me as the
    apple of an eye")

ANTIPHON AND *NUNC DIMITTIS*:
("Lord, now let your servant depart in peace")

KYRIE ELEISON, *Christe eleison, Kyrie eleison*

LORD'S PRAYER: said silently

CREED: said silently

RESPONSES: "Blessed are you, Lord God of our Fathers . . ."

PRAYER: *Visita, quaesumus, Domine*
("Visit, O Lord, this place . . .")

FINAL RESPONSES AND BLESSING

MARIAN ANTIPHON: for the season

Wherever Compline was chanted in the Roman Catholic Church outside of the monastery in a corporate "choral" setting up to 1962, especially cathedral churches and seminaries or other large gatherings, it would have been according to the above order.[108] The various monasteries would also have followed the same plan, but in a simpler form, according to their particular use.[109]

Compline in English and the Oxford Movement

At the end of the sixteenth century, an uneasy peace prevailed in the Church of England. Both Protestant and Catholic extremists had to seek exile on the Continent or America. Catholics who remained in England or

Ireland had to practice their faith in secret. During this time of religious conflict and eventual civil war, a group of theologians in the Church of England known now as the "Caroline Divines" contributed insightful writing on such subjects as salvation, transubstantiation, and beauty, maintaining the Anglican Church's place as a *via media* between Puritan and Catholic causes. From this period comes a book of prayers published by John Cosin in 1627 called *Collection of Private Devotions in the Practice of the Ancient Church, called The Hours of Prayer.* Based on the Latin books of hours, it contained English versions of the Divine Office, including Compline. It was not a strict translation, but quoted many Compline texts, including six verses of Psalm 90 (91), the "Song of Symeon," and several of the prayers.

Richard Challonder (1691–1781) made a major contribution to the Divine Office and Compline; his long life spans most of the period between the Caroline Divines and nineteenth-century Anglo-Catholics. Born in Sussex, he was baptized a Catholic at the age of thirteen, and shortly after enrolled in the English College at Douai, a center for English-speaking Catholics abroad. He was ordained a priest in 1714 and became professor of theology at the college. He went back to England in 1730 and authored a number of works, including a revision of the Douai Rheims Bible (which provided the basis for all English Catholic bibles for the next two hundred years) and a Catholic prayer book called *The Garden of the Soul* (1740), which contained the entire *Officium Divinum* translated into English.[110]

In the early nineteenth century, the modern Anglo-Catholic movement began with a group of writers, many from Oxford, known today as the Oxford Movement or Tractarians (from their publications called *Tracts for the Times*). Perhaps the most well-known Tractarian, John Henry Newman (1801–90), wrote, in 1836, *Tract Number Seventy-Five: On the Roman Breviary as Embodying the Substance of the Devotional Services of the Church Catholic.* As an illustration of his theme, he composed a translation of a whole day's office from the Roman breviary, including Compline.

Newman's tract began a whole series of translations of the offices into English, especially needed for the new orders of Anglican monks and nuns that began forming in the mid-nineteenth century. Of many breviaries, one of the most popular was H. P. Liddon's *The Day Hours of the Church of England,* which went through five editions from 1858 through 1891, and then five printings of a new edition from 1914 through 1931.[111] Scholars began to base this and many other breviaries on their research of the Sarum Antiphonal, England's own pre-Reformation Divine Office.

The beginning of the twentieth century saw two outstanding versions of Compline—one Roman and one Anglican. Both the *Officium Divinum* version of Pius X and the Anglican breviary version were the result of great scholarship and based on centuries-old tradition. The parts of the offices were the same, and differed only in a few details of order, and in the omission of the Marian Antiphon from the Anglican version. But one might argue that these distinguishing features, rooted for the most part in its Sarum past, argued well for the English version of Compline to be considered for inclusion in the proposed Book of Common Prayer of 1928.

✳ ✳ ✳

In my second year at college I took a required course in the history of Western music. The course began with Gregorian chant, and I was excited to learn about the origins of the chants that I had been singing the previous year at Compline.

One of my classmates was older than the rest of us—a Catholic Jesuit priest doing graduate work—I just knew him as Fr. Pierre. I told him about my singing Compline at St. Mark's Cathedral, and I'm sure he recognized my interest in the chant, because the next day he came to class, he had brought me a book: the three-inch-thick Liber Usualis, *the compendium of all the main chants for the Mass and the office.*

I was stunned—here was the best collection of chants—how could Fr. Pierre part with it? "Oh, we're not doing the chants anymore," he replied. "All these books are languishing. Put it to good use!" And I have, ever since. Now, almost fifty years later, with some churches celebrating the pre-1962 Mass, I'm using my "Liber" more than ever.

Vatican II and Night Prayer

The Second Vatican Council, convened by Pope John XXIII, took place from 1963 to 1965. One of the results of the work of the council was a new order of Mass, promulgated by Pope Paul VI in 1969 and published in 1970 (known as the Mass of Paul VI or *Novus Ordo Missae*). In the years immediately following the council, many countries, including the United States, were eager to translate the new Mass into the vernacular, and they received permission to do so from Rome. Although the *Novus Ordo* could be celebrated in its original Latin with all the Gregorian chants intact, most Masses in the United States since the late 1960s have been in English, and the wonderful chants were no longer sung by choirs.[112]

There was already a revision of the Divine Office underway before Vatican II began, but it was not completed until 1970, and an English translation, renamed the Liturgy of the Hours, was published in 1974. The most notable changes were the elimination of the Office of Prime, a decrease in the number of psalms, and the renaming of the other offices.[113]

Compline, renamed Night Prayer, is rearranged and simplified from Pius X's Compline.[114] It begins simply with "O God, come to my assistance," followed by an examination of conscience and a hymn. Psalms 4 and 133 (134) are appointed for Night Prayer after First Vespers of Sunday (Saturday evening), and Psalm 90 (91) is for Second Vespers of Sunday (Sunday evening). There are also specific psalms appointed for the other days of the week. The following table compares the psalms for the days of the week for Compline in the Pius X breviary and Night Prayer in the Liturgy of the Hours.

	PIUS X BREVIARY (old psalm numbering)	LITURGY OF THE HOURS (new psalm numbering)
Sunday	Psalm 4, 90, 133	Psalm 4, 134
Monday	Psalm 6, 7(i), 7(ii)	Psalm 86
Tuesday	Psalm 11, 12, 15	Psalm 143
Wednesday	Psalm 33(i), 33(ii), 60	Psalm 130
Thursday	Psalm 69, 70(i), 70(ii)	Psalm 16
Friday	Psalm 76(i), 76(ii), 85	Psalm 88
Saturday	Psalm 87, 102(i), 102(ii)	Psalm 91

The psalms are followed by a chapter reading and the response "Into your hands, Lord, I commend my spirit." Next is the Song of Simeon, followed by the prayer of the day, a concluding blessing, and the appropriate Marian antiphon.

Compline in Seattle and Non-Catholic
Versions in the 1970s

In the mid-twentieth century in the United States, Compline was not widely known among non-Catholics. Even among the Catholic laity who knew of it, it was something done by those in the religious life (monks, nuns, clergy, and seminarians). Some Catholics may have been fortunate enough to sing Compline or hear it sung on occasion in large parishes or cathedrals. In the 1950s, Catholics and Protestants did not know much of the practice in each other's churches. However, there was one exception: church musicians. A choir director or organist working with a choir singing chant for High Mass in church or school (from a choir loft or behind a screen) might have been a non-Catholic. And these musicians received their training in colleges where Gregorian chant and the liturgy of the Mass and office was taught in music history courses, since chant was the source of Western polyphonic music.

For the non-Catholic laity, two factors helped make the Divine Offices more widely known from 1950 throughout the rest of the twentieth century: liturgical scholarship and popular writings in spirituality. There was great interest in modeling contemporary worship after the early church, and new research was showing that the laity had been active in daily offices during the first three centuries, before fixed-hour prayer became the province of monastics or the clergy. Also, Thomas Merton, who gained national recognition with the publication of *The Seven Storey Mountain* in 1948, was giving readers a look into monastic and contemplative life, which included daily prayer at specific times.

Enter a young organist and choirmaster, Peter Hallock, who started his work in 1951 at St. Mark's Episcopal Cathedral in Seattle, fresh from the Royal School of Church Music in Canterbury. At the time, St. Mark's, the cavernous "Holy Box," had become by default the church venue in Seattle with the best acoustics for chant, since the year before, the Catholic cathedral, St. James, had installed carpet and acoustical tile.[115] It was not surprising, then, that when Hallock offered a class to learn how to sing and read Gregorian Chant in the fall of 1955, a number of men turned out. As he relates, when the class was nearing an end, he used the Office of Compline that he had sung at Canterbury as a kind of "final exam."

When in the spring of 1956 Peter Hallock invited his former chant students and other interested musicians to sing in a group weekly, using Compline as a format, it was this motivating love of chant and choral music that was key; in fact, religion was not a determining factor for membership (and never has been). There was another factor in play, however, which I would call the "British choral ethos." A beautiful anthem, appropriate to the season, was a religious experience in itself—and combined with the themes of Compline, began to draw people to the services, and word quickly spread in Episcopal and Lutheran circles.

Two compositions by Peter Hallock, written during the early 1970s, remind me both of the aesthetic and spiritual experience of Compline at a time when so much interest was growing nationally in the Seattle Compline service. The "Lamentations of Jeremiah" (Listen: example 20) for choir and solo cello, is an anthem for the Lenten season, and usually sung on Palm Sunday. Its text was mostly from the Office of Matins during the last part of Holy Week. The "Easter Canticle" (Listen: example 21) is sung as the choir processes in to sing Compline on Easter Day. These two compositions represent several things for me: the aesthetic and liturgical "highs and lows" that depend on the particular season of the year, and also the reminder of the "British ethos," since the medieval Sarum liturgy favored elaborate processions and anthems.

Compline appeared in prayer books of both the Episcopal and Lutheran churches at the end of the 1970s.[116] The spirit of ecumenism engendered by Vatican II had a definite influence on these new versions of Compline, because both are similar in style and content to Catholic Night Prayer from the 1974 Liturgy of the Hours. Most noticeably, the examination of conscience (confession of sin) is toward the beginning in all three versions, and the Gospel Canticle (Song of Simeon) is now toward the conclusion of the office.[117] Both the Episcopal and Lutheran versions contain a number of psalms, out of which one or more may be selected. (The traditional Compline psalms, 4, 91, and 134, are available in either version.) There are also alternate chapter readings and prayers. The versions of Night Prayer and Lutheran and Episcopal Compline may be compared in the following table.

NIGHT PRAYER, LITURGY OF THE HOURS (1975)	COMPLINE, LUTHERAN BOOK OF WORSHIP (1978)	COMPLINE, THE BOOK OF COMMON PRAYER (1979)
Introductory Sentences	Introductory Sentences	Introductory Sentences
Examination of Conscience	Hymn	Examination of Conscience
Hymn	Examination of Conscience	
Psalm(s)	Psalm(s)	Psalm(s)
Chapter Reading	Chapter Reading	Chapter Reading
Response "Into your hands"	Response "Into your hands"	
	Hymn	Hymn
	Responses including "Keep me as the apple"	Response "Into your hands" and "Keep me as the apple"
	Prayer(s) of the Day	"Lord have mercy"
	Lord's Prayer	Lord's Prayer
		Prayer(s) of the Day
Song of Simeon	Song of Simeon	Song of Simeon
Prayer(s) of the Day		
Concluding Prayers and Blessing	Concluding Prayers and Blessing	Concluding Prayers and Blessing
Marian Antiphon		

Fixed-Hour Prayer: New Versions of Compline

In the 1980s, Compline or Night Prayer became increasingly known among Christians in the United States through the prayer books of the Catholic, Anglican, and Lutheran churches. Not only was it now available to individuals for their private prayer, but it was also suitable for small groups to pray together weekly or monthly, or at a particular time of year, especially Advent or Lent. Also, choirs modeled after Seattle's Compline Choir were formed, in Honolulu (1976), Austin (1985), and Pittsburgh (1988). A book of prayers, compiled by Jim Cotter, *Prayer at Night's Approaching*, was published in 1983, and became very popular.[118] It drew not only on standard Compline prayers but also on other prayers appropriate to the close of day. The end of the decade saw the publication of *A New Zealand Prayer Book* (1989). The language of this book was poetic, showing a change in sensitivity to such things as inclusion of indigenous cultures and gender neutrality. The elements of Compline were presented in sections with evocative titles, such as "Approach," "Invocation," or "Sentence of the Day"—along with the standard "Psalm" or "Reading."

The 1990s saw a growing number of books of and about the Divine Offices and Compline, not only from various Christian denominations but also from individual authors. In 1992, Anglican Franciscans published *Celebrating Common Prayer*, and Night Prayer was also part of the Presbyterian Church's *Book of Common Worship* (1993) and the United Methodist Church's *The Book of Offices and Services* (1994).

In 1996 the Northumbria Community published *Celtic Night Prayer*—a Compline for each day of the week, named after a different Celtic saint, which did not follow any of the traditional structures. That same year, Kathleen Norris's *The Cloister Walk* was published, describing her time residing at a Benedictine monastery and generating great interest in monastic spirituality and the life of prayer. In the next several years, two books explored the practice and nature of the Divine Hours: Cynthia Bourgeault's *Singing the Psalms* (1997) and David Steindl-Rast and Sharon Lebell's *Music of Silence* (1998, with a foreword by Kathleen Norris). By the end of the decade, a new communications media— the Internet—was in full swing. I helped to create the first website for the Compline Choir in 1998. The choirs in the United States and Canada singing Compline by the end of the decade of the 1990s probably numbered about twenty.

As the twenty-first century dawned, the number of books of or about fixed-hour prayer continued to appear with great frequency. The Church of England finally revised its book of prayer, called *Common Worship* (2000), and published Night Prayer in both traditional and contemporary language. This new version put the confession and hymn toward the beginning as in the Liturgy of the Hours, but left the *Nunc dimittis* in its former place before the prayers. Several lengthy sets of responses were eliminated; otherwise, Night Prayer in the traditional language is equivalent to the 1928 version of Compline (see appendix A).

In 2000 in the United States several prayer books appeared that were definitely new containers for the "old wine" of daily prayer. Simple, easy to use, but encompassing the main elements of the offices, these collections have had a great appeal to a wider audience of Christians who are rediscovering fixed-hour prayer as an ancient practice. Both Robert Benson's *Venite: A Book of Daily Prayer* and Phyllis Tickle's *The Divine Hours* provide for four daily prayer times: morning, noon, evening, and before sleep. Benson's offices are only presented once, but there is provision for variation in the readings and psalms. Tickle's *Divine Hours* are in three volumes, and, in a given volume (like *Prayers for Summertime*) one prays the same Compline for each weekday in a given month; this allows for seven different variations in the readings and psalms for Compline during that month. One of the most practical features in *The Divine Hours* is that each office is complete unto itself, and one does not have to flip pages to look somewhere else in the book for a given reading or psalm.

The last decade has seen many publications enriching the practice of fixed-hour prayer, and many of these are listed in appendix C. But perhaps the most significant trend since 2000 is the proliferation of websites for the offices. Today, I can switch on my tablet computer, press a saved Internet site, and instantly be viewing Morning Prayer for today's date from the Liturgy of the Hours. The use of e-books for tablets or smartphones also makes individual prayer of the offices very easy. And the choices today are amazing, having led not only to the availability of modern offices but also to the ability to pray older ones. One website displays the *Officium Divinum* in its 1570, Pius X, or 1960 versions, with English translation.[119] I have listed these online resources at the beginning of appendix C.

The Future: What's Next?

We have been the beneficiaries of an information explosion, and it will continue to expand and extend our access to data. Websites and their related applications like Facebook, YouTube, and Twitter (and whatever will be invented next) will continue to improve both our communication about Compline and our communities dedicated to praying the Divine Offices. Some work has been done in recent years to have live audio and even video of the Divine Hours. (A Seattle group called the Byrd Ensemble, for instance, has streamed live video of their singing of Compline.)

At St. Mark's in Seattle, Compline is still sung every Sunday, and the choir has a full roster of singers with an average age much lower than in years past. The weekly broadcast and live streaming to thousands of listeners may soon become available nationally. And the choir is exploring how we, with St. Mark's Cathedral, can connect better with the Compline attendees, through a phone app and other means.

There are more ways than ever to observe the fixed hours of prayer, and I'm sure more to come. But if one wants to start praying the office, I really like this advice from Robert Benson: "Begin with one Office, the one that speaks to you most clearly, and work with it for a time until it has become part of your habit."[120]

FOR FURTHER READING

Benson, Robert. *In Constant Prayer (Ancient Practices Series)* Nashville: Thomas Nelson, 2008.

Boers, Arthur Paul. *The Rhythm of God's Grace.* Brewster, MA: Paraclete Press, 2003.

McKnight, Scot. *Praying with the Church: Following Jesus Daily, Hourly, Today.* Brewster, MA: Paraclete Press, 2006.

Taft, Robert. *The Liturgy of the Hours in East and West.* Collegeville, MN: Liturgical Press, 1993.

Compline Choir, St. Mark's Cathedral, Seattle

Gabrielle Fine, 2009

11

The Monks of Broadway

COMMUNITY

Alone, I am what I am, but in community I have the chance to
become everything that I can be.

—JOAN CHITTISTER[121]

* * *

Seattle's St. Mark's Cathedral, like many sacred spaces,
sits atop a hill. If you were to walk south along the
street fronting the cathedral, you would soon come to
the Broadway area of Capitol Hill, which has long been
one of Seattle's centers of youth culture and hip fashion.
The closeness of Broadway to St. Mark's no doubt brought
many young people to the Compline service in the mid-
1960s, and nurtures the continuing tradition today. It has
also influenced the ministries of the cathedral parish to the
people in the Broadway district—especially to the homeless.
I was amused but not too surprised when, in the 1970s,
someone referred to the Compline Choir as "The Monks
of Broadway." But this was the moment I started wondering

about our mission to ourselves and our attendees—if not exactly monks, what were we?

✳   ✳   ✳

It was 1969, a dark fall Sunday evening in Seattle. The Compline Choir was rehearsing in the choir room, when Roxy Giddings, the wife of one of our members, suddenly opened the door and came into the room. She said simply, "There's a naked woman sitting in the bishop's throne. Can anyone help?"

In the 1960s, in the west end of St. Mark's Cathedral, there was a raised area with a freestanding altar, directly behind which was the bishop's chair. As the symbol of the presence of the bishop (the "cathedra," from which "cathedral" gets its name), this chair could aptly be called a throne; it was about six feet high, with fine upholstery and elaborately carved woodwork—faces at the ends of the arms and a knight's visored head at the top.

Ralph Carskadden, an Episcopal priest who was singing with us at the time, answered Roxy's plea for help. They approached the naked young woman, who was apparently high on some kind of drug. She had decided to remove her wet clothes and seek the comfort of the large, soft chair, which was hidden from view behind the altar. Ralph found a blanket, and they covered her with it and escorted her to a restroom, where Roxy helped her to get her clothes back on.

The story of the naked woman at Compline always reminds me of the openness and hospitality shown by two communities—the Compline Choir and St. Mark's Episcopal Cathedral—to the weekly gathering of attendees. It also speaks of the unique and long-standing relationship of the choir and St. Mark's in creating and maintaining the Compline service. Living out one's spiritual path in a community is an important part of the journey, and I would like to examine the community of the Compline Choir as an example of what we can learn about this essential component of spirituality.

What does the word *community* mean exactly? The word is often applied today to denote a group of people that share some common characteristic or interest—such as calling those who attend the Compline service the "Compline Community." But I would like to define *community* as what takes place when people that have a common interest begin to communicate with each other and organize their group to achieve a common goal. Beginning with a specific vision, a community articulates its mission and organizes to carry it out; once formed, it needs to revisit and refine its mission in order to remain vibrant and alive.

The evolution of the Compline Choir is an example of the continuing re-formation of a vision and mission over the decades of its existence. The group began as a group of men interested in singing, most of whose members did not belong to the St. Mark's congregation; they sang a monastic office once a week for their own musical and spiritual edification. Without losing this core purpose, the service they sang was always open to attendees—but after the radio broadcasts began, and the Flower Children of the 1960s discovered Compline, there was a new aspect of ministry to the choir's mission. A great variety of texts, in the form of psalms, hymns, and anthems were sung, now for what they might offer not only to the choir but also to the attendees—some of whom discovered and joined the St. Mark's Episcopal Cathedral community. In the 1980s, the boundaries between the choir and the cathedral needed definition, and the Compline Choir maintained its autonomy by becoming its own nonprofit organization. In the last decade, the cathedral community has provided volunteer greeters, and both communities continue to improve their complementary roles in a shared Compline ministry.

Benedictine Values in Community

In his book *The Different Drum: Community Making and Peace*, M. Scott Peck mentions a number of factors crucial to "community maintenance."[122] We can also learn much about community dynamics by studying the model established by the *Rule of Benedict*, which has had an influence over thousands of communities for over fifteen hundred years. I would like to discuss each of the factors given by Peck, and relate them to corresponding parts of Benedict's Rule.

Commitment

Some degree of commitment is necessary for any community, and there must be enough people to provide the resources needed to make the community prosper. The Compline Choir requires a high level of commitment, since it sings the office every Sunday of the year and also at special events. One of the main vows of a Benedictine monastic as well as oblates (lay associates) is that of *stability*, the commitment to a particular community. But unlike the oblate, who makes a lifetime commitment, the members of the Compline Choir make an annual commitment to sing a particular number of Sundays per year.

Authority

Every community has some form of leadership model, and must work smoothly within that model. The Compline Choir has a board of directors with legal authority, but the artistic director is the leader for all matters regarding the performance of the music. There is also an additional quality of leadership, similar to monastic orders, where the leader functions, as described by Joan Chittister, as "a spiritual parent" to lead individuals "to spiritual adulthood where they themselves make the kind of choices that give life depth and quality."[123] This role, which was articulated by the choir's founder, Peter Hallock, stimulated and encouraged a sense of personal involvement, commitment, and passion for the group.

Structure

It is important for every organization to have specific roles for members. When these are shared widely, ownership is spread throughout the group. The Rule of Benedict, in addition to describing particular roles within a monastery, contains what I would call the lubrication of a "well-oiled machine": the art of listening. In a monastery, all, especially the leader, are listening "with the ear of the heart" to where God is leading them. Communities would do well to listen: to each other and to where their vision and mission are leading them.

Ritual

All communities have some form of ritual, to solidify their mission and maintain morale. The Compline Choir's main mission is to sing a Divine Office, a ritual in itself, but many little rituals and traditions have built up over the decades to strengthen and solidify our community. For example, having a number of tasks that get done automatically, such as recording the podcast, updating the web page with the weekly service music, knowing when it is one's turn to be the reader or cantor, and observing the ritual of silence before we go into the church—all these little tasks help the group function efficiently to fulfill our mission. Also, music and ritual are important cocreators of our spirituality, even though the beliefs of individual members range from Roman Catholic to atheist. On music, Russill Paul writes, "Life has a vital sonic dimension that colors our moods and sentiments, our joys and fears, our love and pain."[124]

Other Factors

Peck mentions a number of other factors important to a group's formation and its evolution over time; these include size, task definition, inclusivity, intensity, and individuality. As one or more of these become issues over time, the critical question is one of balance, as Joan Chittister observes: "When we go to excess in one dimension of life, the unbalance in something else destroys us. Work, for instance, is good, but not at the expense of family. Love is good, but not at the expense of work."[125] If a particular factor gets out of balance, it can affect the mission of the community. For example, if the Compline Choir became more inclusive by not auditioning its members, then either it would have to sing less challenging music or lengthen rehearsal time. Another challenge, the aging of its members, was successfully met by recruiting young, talented singers, and now it looks like the choir can go on for another fifty years.

Other Values That Enhance Community

One of the main values from the Rule of Benedict is love or compassion. Thomas Merton, who was influenced by Buddhism, wrote that "compassion is the keen awareness of the interdependence of all things."[126] We all feel isolated at times—we even give expression to this when we sing the spiritual "Sometimes I feel like a motherless child" (Listen: example 22). When we have empathy and compassion, we no longer feel isolated, and we realize that we are the instruments of God's work in the world.

Chapter 4 of Benedict's Rule, "The Tools for Good Works," lists a number of virtues, including zeal, patience, perseverance, moderation and balance, self-discipline, reverence, joy, justice, and peace.[127] Another quality, humility, has its own section in the Rule, and is composed of twelve steps, envisioned on a ladder, where we have to descend from ego and self-importance in order to ascend to heaven. Another Benedictine virtue, hospitality, is a result of the recognition that God's face is that of each other. St. Benedict wrote, "Let all guests who arrive be received like Christ."[128] These tools, so important to community-building, all proceed from compassion or love.

Pilgrimages

One of the ways a community that does not live together can strengthen its mission is to travel on a tour or pilgrimage. It is a chance also for members to spend more time together, learn about each other, and grow more deeply as a community.

✳ ✳ ✳

In July of 1997 the Compline Choir traveled to Russia and Scandinavia to sing Compline in several places and especially to listen to Russian Orthodox music. We arrived at the Orthodox seminary in St. Petersburg, jet-lagged but excited. After getting settled, and fortifying ourselves with some tea and biscuits in the seminary's dining room, we walked from the seminary, past the Alexander Nevsky Monastery, to the Tikhvin Cemetery.

In one corner of the cemetery, called the Composers' Corner, are buried some of the most influential Russian composers of the nineteenth century—among them Tchaikovsky, Mussorgsky, and Rimsky-Korsakov. We gathered together and sang the "Kievan Kontakion":

> *Give rest, O Christ, to your servant with your saints,*
> *where sorrow and pain are no more,*
> *neither sighing but life everlasting.*

In spite of being tired, I was extremely moved. Our group, one of whose main purposes was to encounter beauty, was paying homage to composers who had brought forth such incredible beauty into the world; I felt that we were affirming our part in that larger community, with those masters who had gone before.

The Compline Choir has made several other major trips over its existence, including a tour of England in the summer of 2000. It was an opportunity not only to sing our office in several English cathedrals but also to steep ourselves in a culture that provided the roots for our own.

Those Gone Before

As communities evolve over the years, the list of deceased members grows. In a group like the Compline Choir, these are our most immediate "saints." Their contribution to the community lives on in in memory and shared story, but perhaps more importantly in the culture and fabric of the group that they have formed. I would like to mention three such members who have been exemplars for me.

Charles H. Sherwood (1909–97) was my mentor in the tenor section from the time I met him in 1964. He was born of English parents who had immigrated to Victoria, British Columbia, and had developed a commanding "quasi-British" voice that stood him well as the reader for the Compline service and deservedly earned him the title "The Voice of God." In World War II he had served with the Royal Canadian Air Force, and when his bomber was shot down over enemy lines, he was smuggled out by the Underground through France and Spain. He immigrated to Seattle and managed the sheet music department at Seattle's largest music store; he was always finding the Compline Choir pieces to sing and giving us little educational handouts, such as a sheet (which I still have) that shows where all the verses in the Lamentations of Jeremiah come from in the chants for Holy Week offices. Although an Anglican, he directed Roman Catholic choirs for more than forty years.

Winfield Tudor (1918–2002) was born in Barbados, West Indies, and sang at the age of ten in the St. Michael's choir there. He learned the printing trade from an uncle and after immigrating to Seattle in 1948 became the first African American printer at the *Seattle Times*, retiring after forty-three years—fortunately just when typesetting was becoming obsolete. I hardly remember Winfield ever being absent from Compline. He and his wife, Doreen, hosted an annual Christmas party for the Compline Choir, where Barbadian rum flowed in abundance. The annual party still goes on, now in Winfield's memory.

James D. Holloway (1960–2001) sang with the Compline Choir only for a few years in the 1990s but made a lasting impression on the group with his amazing talent as a pianist and organist, and his verve and sense of humor. Tragically, he was shot and killed at random in May 2001 on the Pacific Lutheran University campus by a deranged person, who then took his own life. At the time Jim was university organist and professor of organ and church music at PLU. At the Compline service the following Sunday, which was dedicated to Jim, we sang as the hymn "Jerusalem, My Happy Home" (Listen: example 23). One of its verses is particularly meaningful to our community of musicians; it speaks of the heavenly choir, led by King David, who has always been credited with composing many of the psalms. It reminds us that in community, the music made by individual members resounds in our lives and will be there in the life to come.

There David stands with harp in hand
As master of the choir:

Ten thousand times that one were blest
That might this music hear.

FOR FURTHER READING

Chittister, Joan D., OSB. *The Rule of Benedict: Insights for the Ages.*
New York: Crossroad, 1992. 2nd ed.: *The Rule of Benedict: A
Spirituality for the 21st Century.* New York: Crossroad, 2010.

————. *Wisdom Distilled from the Daily: Living the Rule of St.
Benedict Today.* San Francisco: HarperSanFrancisco, 1990.

Peck, M. Scott. *The Different Drum: Community Making and
Peace.* New York: Simon & Schuster, 1987.

Woman on Labyrinth, St. Mark's Cathedral, Seattle   Gabrielle Fine, 2009

12

In the Shadow of Your Wings

FINDING LASTING PEACE

For it is Thou, O Lord, that makest us dwell in safety.

—*ORDER OF COMPLINE, FINAL RESPONSE*[129]

* * *

The sun had set as we waited outside the north transept of the Cathedral of Notre Dame de Chartres. I had come to Europe in May of 1999 on a pilgrimage that would take me through France, Italy, and Germany. On my arrival I attended a workshop about the Chartres Labyrinth, an ancient pattern on the floor near the entrance of the cathedral, which had been navigated by pilgrims in the Middle Ages and rediscovered in the late twentieth century as a tool for spiritual growth.

The doors to the cathedral, closed after the last tourist had been ushered out for the day, were opened to allow us exclusive use of the labyrinth. As we entered, we were each given a single red rose to carry, a symbol of the Virgin Mary. Awed by the silence and emptiness of the

*great edifice, I made my way to the West Portal, where, underneath
the rose window, the labyrinth was waiting, dimly lit by candles.*

We come to Compline seeking many things—
communion, forgiveness, strength, enlightenment—
but perhaps most of all we come to find peace. In its most
elemental form, peace is protection and safety from harm.
But we also seek release from pain, anxiety, and from fears
of many kinds—such as failure or death. At the end of the
day, we pray to let go of our cares, fold ourselves under the
wings of the Divine Presence, and enter into a quiet night.

One of the parts of Compline that speaks of lasting peace is
Psalm 90 (91) (Listen: example 3). It is one of the appointed
psalms for Compline not just because it refers to "terror by
night" but also because it describes the peace that comes
within the resting presence of God, as in these verses:

> He who dwells in the shelter of the Most High, *
>> abides under the shadow of the Almighty.
> He shall say to the LORD, "You are my refuge and my
>> stronghold, *
>> my God in whom I put my trust."
> He shall deliver you from the snare of the hunter *
>> and from the deadly pestilence.
> He shall cover you with his pinions, and you shall find
>> refuge under his wings; *
>> his faithfulness shall be a shield and buckler.

. . .

Because he is bound to me in love, therefore will I
　deliver him; *
I will protect him, because he knows my Name.[130]

In the last of the verses above, God speaks of a great
covenant: because we know the name of the Nameless One,
and are bound together in love and faith, we will be safe from
harm. This divine peace is expressed in a vision of guardian
angels, and in the Shekhinah—the nurturing, maternal
presence—the feminine aspect of the divine.

✳　✳　✳

*As pilgrims had done since 1200, I stepped onto the labyrinth to
begin my meditative path to the center. As I walked, I held my rose,
but I also carried my particular concerns for this walk: my recent
divorce, the pain of a love affair that had ended, and my role as an
only child in the care of my mother, whose dementia was worsening.
Each step took me further and further into stillness, toward a place
of peace.*

*A group of four singers had come down from Paris to provide music
to accompany our walk. They began with something that I recognized
as very appropriate: a fourteenth-century pilgrim song from Santa
Maria de Montserrat—which, like Chartres, was dedicated to
Mary and revered for its black Madonna. The song began "O Virgo
splendes":*

O resplendent Virgin,
here on the high mountain of shining wonders
which all the faithful ascend,
behold them with your merciful eye of peace.

A walk on the labyrinth, is, like Compline, a contemplative spiritual experience that opens me up to the same resting presence in the divine, the peace of God. This protective presence is best described in more "feminine/yin/night" terms than those of "masculine/yang/day." To come to a greater understanding of the elements the labyrinth has in common with Compline, I would like to take a look at several features of this ancient form.

The labyrinth pattern is over four thousand years old and appears in many of the world's cultures. In the Grecian myth, Theseus goes through the Cretan labyrinth to do battle with a monster and then finds his way back using the thread given him by Ariadne, which he had unwound behind him on his journey. The Cretan labyrinth had many blind alleys, and today would be called a maze; the word *labyrinth* is now commonly used to describe a path that is *unicursal* (having only one way to and from the center). It is this form that began to be imprinted on the floors of European churches and cathedrals in the twelfth through the fourteenth centuries. Lauren Artress writes that a maze, with its problems to be solved, engages our thinking minds, while a labyrinth "invites our intuitive, pattern-seeking, symbolic mind to come forth."[131] One who walks on the labyrinth walks a sacred path, a metaphor of the spiritual journey.

The Chartres labyrinth has many numerological and symbolic features, several of which are relevant here. The eleven concentric circles represent the cosmos as understood by medieval scholars, with the earth at the center. The first seven rings represent the moon, sun, and known planets. The eighth ring represents the celestial sphere of the stars and zodiac. Rings nine through eleven represent World Soul, Mind, and Supreme God.[132] The center of the labyrinth is a six-petaled rose and is a Christian symbol of both the Holy Spirit and the Virgin Mary. By the end of the twelfth century, when the labyrinth was constructed, it was also regarded as a symbol for Mary, like the rose window above it.

Two elements of Compline remind me of the labyrinth. The eighth circle (the celestial sphere) is brought to mind by the oldest of the Compline prayers, said before the close of the office, invoking the angels as agents and messengers of God to protect us and keep us safe. It was also a personal prayer asking God's blessing and protection over a monastic house: "Visit, this place, O Lord, and drive far from it all snares of the enemy; let your holy angels dwell with us to preserve us in peace; and let your blessing be upon us always; through Jesus Christ our Lord. Amen."[133] The other element is the anthem to Mary that comes at the end of Compline, said or sung since medieval times in the Roman Catholic Church. Before describing this in greater detail, suffice it to say that in the Middle Ages, Christians in the Latin West began to regard Mary as the Queen of Heaven—chief among the angels. This sentiment is perhaps best captured in the first two verses of the hymn "Ye watchers and ye holy ones."[134] I had sung this for years without thinking about the meaning of the second verse and realizing it was all about Mary:

> Ye watchers and ye holy ones,
> Bright seraphs, cherubim and thrones,
> Raise the glad strain, Alleluia!
> Cry out, dominions, princedoms, powers,
> Virtues, archangels, angels' choirs:
> Alleluia! Alleluia! Alleluia! Alleluia! Alleluia!

O higher than the cherubim,
More glorious than the seraphim,
Lead their praises, Alleluia!
Thou bearer of th'eternal Word,
Most gracious, magnify the Lord.
Alleluia! Alleluia! Alleluia! Alleluia! Alleluia!

The angels, and their heavenly Queen become the symbols and guardians of our protective relationship with the divine.

✳ ✳ ✳

Once on the labyrinth journey, I only needed to focus on the path ahead—but it was easy to be distracted by unexpected meetings with other people, or listening too deeply to the music. However, I soon reached a state of balance, taking each turn as a new surprise, and letting go of time as I navigated Mary's web to the center. I also let go of my troubling thoughts, trusting that whatever answer I needed at this moment would come.

David Steindl-Rast and Sharon Lebell, in their book *Music of Silence*, assign a particular virtue to each of the Divine Hours; the virtue for Compline is *faith*. As we come to the end of the day, "Compline encourages us to see with the eyes of trust that the cosmos is in fact prepared for us, like a nurturing home."[135] The labyrinth, as map of the universe, represents to those who enter its confines this enfolding, protective relationship. Interestingly, I had a very bad experience once where I didn't feel worthy enough to join other people on their walk; I sat by the side of the labyrinth and wept. The labyrinth becomes a litmus test of our inner processes; when we focus entirely on ourselves, a spiritual breakthrough is impossible. Steindl-Rast and Lebell say that the choice "to live in basic trust, to see the universe as the home that God has made for us, or to live in fear and distrust, is ultimately ours."[136] Compline reminds us to face our fears, give thanks for our protection from harm, and pray for restful sleep and good dreams, releasing our trust to the Almighty.

*   *   *

As always, I was surprised to take the final turn before entering the center of the labyrinth, with its six petals. I stepped into one of the unoccupied spaces, and stood, expressing thanks for my journey. I became especially grateful for my mother's life, and all the love she had given me. But now it seemed as though she hardly knew me— she was already moving quickly to her new destination. Suddenly, surrounded by all the symbols of Mary, I felt a new kind of acceptance of her, not only as Universal Mother and symbol of ultimate trust and faith, but as a surrogate, a mother, for me, directly. I clasped my rose a little more tightly.

During the Middle Ages it became customary in monasteries to sing an antiphon to the Virgin Mary at the end of Lauds and Compline, often in a special chapel dedicated to Mary (sometimes called the "Lady Chapel"). The "Marian Antiphon," as it is known, has also been sung at the end of Compline in the Roman Catholic tradition outside of monasteries, and is still true of Catholic Night Prayer today. It is very moving to attend Compline in a monastery, and hear the singing of one of the hymns to Mary appropriate to the season, after which the abbot or prioress gives the blessing over the house, sprinkling all with holy water. David Steindl-Rast and Sharon Lebell's observations are worth quoting here:

> This custom has always reminded me of children being tucked into bed at the end of the day by their mother. It brings a smile to my face to think of all these monks sweetly singing at day's end to their Mother, opening themselves to the *anima* realm of their psyche, and entrusting themselves to the infinite darkness as maternal. Thus the part of the monastery indelibly linked for me with Compline is the Lady Chapel, where we return to our spiritual womb to be reborn again next morning.[137]

There are four Marian Antiphons, Gregorian chants sung at the end of Compline at different times of the year:

- *Alma Redemptoris Mater*—from Advent to Purification (February 2)
- *Ave Regina Caelorum*—from Purification to Easter

- *Regina Caeli Laetare*—from Easter to Pentecost
- *Salve Regina*—from Pentecost to Advent

Each of the chants has a simple and a more elaborate version. Here, for example, is the text of the *Salve Regina*, with a musical example of the elaborate version (Listen: example 24).

Salve, Regina, mater
  misericordiae;
vita, dulcedo et spes
  nostra, salve.
Ad te clamamus, exsules
  filii Evae.
Ad te suspiramus,
  gementes et flentes
in hac lacrimarum valle.

Eia ergo, advocata nostra,

illos tuos misericordes
  oculos ad nos converte.
Et Jesum, benedictum
  fructum ventris tui,
nobis post hoc exsilium
  ostende.
O clemens, o pia, o dulcis
  Virgo Maria.

Hail, holy Queen, Mother
  of mercy,
hail, our life, our
  sweetness, and our hope.
To you we cry, the children
  of Eve;
to you we send up our
  sighs,
mourning and weeping in
  this land of exile.

Turn, then, most gracious
  advocate,
your eyes of mercy toward
  us;
lead us home at last

and show us the blessed
  fruit of your womb, Jesus:
O clement, O loving, O
  sweet virgin Mary.

I have chosen to have this musical example chanted by women's voices. It carries us immediately into our "anima" side and the feminine side of the divine.

✳ ✳ ✳

It was time to retrace my steps along the same path that I had traveled into the center. The journey out of the labyrinth is always similar to a kind of rebirth, but my revelation of Mary as Divine Mother made this a birth of peace and joy. I listened again to the men singing fourteenth-century songs, and I thought ahead to the next day, when I would take the train to Solesmes Monastery to spend two days in silent retreat. They sang me on my way, with "Stella splendens in monte . . .":

> Splendid Star on the serrated mountain, with miracles shining like a sunbeam, hear the people. From all around they rally, rejoicing, rich and poor, young and old. They assemble here to see with their own eyes, and return from it filled with grace.

In our time, we are deepening our sense of the feminine face of God. There has been a slow evolution in our thinking over the last five or six decades toward this idea. Carl Jung saw the promulgation of the dogma of the Assumption of the Blessed Virgin Mary in 1950 as a sign of symbolic acknowledgment that divinity was both masculine and feminine.[138] We have been moving toward a greater awareness and integration of the aspects of the Divine Mother: wisdom, compassion, intuition, and nurturing of the planet. Especially the latter—care for the planet—is more urgent now than at the time the following was written (1996): "Unless we wake up to the full reality of what we have done and are doing to the planet, it may be too late to alter the course of events we have unwittingly set in motion. In response to this crisis, the Divine Feminine is activated in the depths of our soul to help us see what needs to be done and to do it."[139]

One last part of Compline that resonates the most with me when I think about finding lasting peace is the short response sung just before the canticle *Nunc dimittis*: "Keep me as the apple of an eye. Hide me under the shadow of Thy wings." This little mantra, which could stand on its own as representative of all of Compline, always says to me something like "God knows us all as unique beings, unique as the imprint of our iris." We need to let ourselves rest in that loving care, under the shadow of the Almighty.

When we enter into that mystical communion with the divine, aware and vigilant, repentant of our sins, resting in the Eternal Presence that is with us and in us all, and found in so much beauty—then we have found all that prayer at the end of the day has to offer. Then, with the psalmist we can say:

> You have put gladness in my heart, *
> > more than when grain and wine and oil increase.
> I lie down in peace; at once I fall asleep; *
> > for only you, LORD, make me dwell in safety.

FOR FURTHER READING

Artress, Lauren. *Walking a Sacred Path: Rediscovering the Labyrinth as a Spiritual Tool.* New York: Riverhead, 1995.

Harvey, Andrew, and Anne Baring. *The Divine Feminine: Exploring the Feminine Face of God Throughout the World.* Berkeley: Conari, 1996.

Jung, Carl. *The Essential Jung.* Selected and edited by Anthony Storr. Princeton: Princeton University Press, 1983.

Steindl-Rast, David, and Sharon Lebell. *Music of Silence: A Sacred Journey Through the Hours of the Day.* Foreword by Kathleen Norris. Berkeley, CA: Seastone, 1998.

Epilogue

It has been my purpose to explore in some depth this wonderful little ritual at the end of the day called Compline or Night Prayer—in history, in my own thoughts and memories, and in musical selections that have carried the greatest meaning for me over the years. Our particular journey together is nearing an end, but I hope some of the thoughts I have expressed will encourage you to find new experiences of the divine mystery.

I have written about the elements of my life with Compline that I think are important to our lifelong spiritual journey: finding some direct experience of the divine, having a sense of vigilance, remembering our mortality, experiencing beauty, and practicing compassion. All of these lead to that experience of peace, which is, after all, the reason why we pray at the close of day. I think I have found some satisfactory answers to the question I asked myself that first night at Compline, almost fifty years ago: "What is going on here?" I'll leave you with that first song (Listen: example 25); it was all there then, as now:

> *Now the day is over,*
> *Night is drawing nigh,*

Shadows of the evening
Steal across the sky.

Jesus, give the weary
Calm and sweet repose;
With Thy tend'rest blessing
May our eyelids close.

Through the long night watches
May Thine angels spread
Their white wings above me,
Watching round my bed.

Acknowledgments

I along with many, many others, am grateful to Peter Hallock for forming the choir that still sings the Office of Compline at St. Mark's Episcopal Cathedral in Seattle, Washington, and for his stellar contribution to church music over many decades. I am also grateful to him for many years as my mentor and friend, as well as for his input into this book.

I thank Joseph Anderson of the Center for Sacred Art in Seattle, as well as Jason Anderson, Compline Choir director, and choir members Paul Johns and Joel Matter, who commented on early drafts of the manuscript. And thanks to John and Nancy Marshall of the Episcopal Bookstore, for also reading an early draft and for guiding me in those early days.

Thanks to Gabrielle Fine, for providing photographic images that give a visual accompaniment to the themes of Compline.

I am grateful to Waverly Fitzgerald for her expertise in coaching me on the art of writing both book and proposal, and for editing (and sometimes reediting) the manuscript.

Kudos to Compline Choir members Derek Tilton, for assistance in producing the musical notation in the chapter on beauty; Layne Benofsky, for production of the website for musical examples; and Joel Matter, for writing the contents of appendix A and proofing the texts and attributions for appendix B. Thanks also to Markdavin Obenza and Joshua Haberman, of Seattle's Byrd Ensemble, not only for several musical examples, but also for editing all the examples through their company, Scribe Records.

Thanks to Alexander Lingas, director, and Mark Powell, executive director, of the group Cappella Romana for the musical example "God is with us," and for helping me learn about Compline in the Byzantine rite.

I also appreciate the help from Bill McJohn, of the Peregrine Medieval Vocal Ensemble, for his translations of collects from the *Bangor Antiphoner*.

Finally I want to thank my wife, Margaret O'Donnell, for her love and encouragement, and for her enthusiasm about this project. She kept me going when this journey seemed too long.

Appendix A

THE OFFICE OF COMPLINE

[Listen along with the words to example 1 on the website www. prayerasnightfalls.com]

[The following is an adaptation of the Order for Compline published by The Plainsong & Mediæval Music Society, copyright © 1949, which itself is based on the text of Compline in *The Book of Common Prayer . . . Proposed in 1928*. Texts of the variable musical selections (Orison, Psalm, Hymn, *Nunc dimittis*, and Anthem) are supplied on the website.]

[A bidding prayer may be read and an orison may be sung. On festival days, a processional may be sung instead of the bidding prayer and orison, or as a prelude to one or both of them.]

✳ ✳ ✳

READER: The Lord Almighty grant us a quiet night and a perfect end.

CHOIR: Amen.

READER: Beloved in Christ, be sober, be vigilant; because your adversary the devil, as a roaring lion, walketh about, seeking whom he may devour:

whom resist, steadfast in the faith. [from 1 Peter
5: 8–9a]

READER: But thou, O Lord, have mercy upon us.

CHOIR: Thanks be to God.

[The following is chanted.]

CANTOR: O God, make speed to save us;

CHOIR: O Lord, make haste to help us.

CANTOR: Glory be to the Father, and to the Son, and to
the Holy Ghost;

CHOIR: As it was in the beginning, is now, and ever shall
be: world without end. Amen.

CANTOR: Praise ye the Lord;

CHOIR: The Lord's name be praiséd.

[A psalm is sung. The appointed psalms for Compline are Psalm 4 (*Cum
invocarem*), Psalm 31:1–6 (*In te, Domine, speravi*), Psalm 91 (*Qui habitat*),
and Psalm 134 (*Ecce nunc*). Other psalms may be used as appropriate to
the church year.]

[A lesson is spoken by the READER, one of the three following choices:]

Thou, O Lord, art in the midst of us, and we are called by
thy name. Leave us not, O Lord our God [from Jeremiah
14:9]

Or

Come unto me, all ye that labour and are heavy laden, and I will give you rest. Take my yoke upon you and learn of me: for I am meek and lowly of heart: and ye shall find rest unto your souls. For my yoke is easy, and my burden is light [from Matthew 11:28–30]

Or

Now the God of peace, that brought again from the dead our Lord Jesus, that great Shepherd of the sheep, through the blood of the Everlasting Covenant, make you perfect in every good work to do his will, working in you that which is well-pleasing in his sight; through Jesus Christ, to whom be glory for ever and ever. Amen. [from Hebrews 13:20–21]

CHOIR: Thanks be to God.

[The following response is chanted:]

CANTOR: Into thy hands, O Lord, I commend my spirit.

CHOIR: Into thy hands, O Lord, I commend my spirit.

CANTOR: For thou hast redeeméd me, O Lord, thou God of truth;

CHOIR: I commend my spirit.

CANTOR: Glory be to the Father, and to the Son, and to the Holy Ghost;

CHOIR: Into thy hands, O Lord, I commend my spirit.

[A hymn is sung. The hymn appointed for Compline is *Te lucis ante terminum* ("Before the ending of the day"). Other hymns may be sung as appropriate to the church year.]

[The following is chanted:]

CANTOR: Keep me as the apple of an eye;

CHOIR: Hide me under the shadow of thy wings.

[A setting of the *Nunc dimittis* (from Luke 2:29–32, plus the *Gloria Patri*) is sung. The text may be from the King James Version or from one of several modern translations. This antiphon precedes and follows it:]

Preserve us, O Lord, while waking, and guard us while sleeping, that awake we may watch with Christ, and asleep we may rest in peace.

Lord, now lettest thou thy servant depart in peace, according to thy word;

For mine eyes have seen thy salvation;

A light to lighten the Gentiles, and the glory of thy people Israel.

Glory be to the Father, and to the Son, and to the Holy Ghost;

As it was in the beginning, is now, and ever shall be, world without end. Amen. [King James Version]

[The Apostles' Creed is intoned by the choir. The congregation rises.]

CANTOR: I believe in God,

CHOIR: the Father almighty,

maker of heaven and earth;

And in Jesus Christ his only Son our Lord,

who was conceived by the Holy Ghost,

born of the Virgin Mary,

suffered under Pontius Pilate,

was crucified, died, and buried.

He descended into hell.

The third day he rose again

and ascended into heaven,

and is seated at the right hand of God the
Father almighty.

From thence he shall come to judge the quick
and the dead.

I believe in the Holy Ghost,

the holy catholic church,

the communion of saints,

the forgiveness of sins,

the resurrection of the body,

and the life everlasting. Amen.

[The congregation is seated. The Kyrie is chanted:]

CANTOR: Lord, have mercy upon us.

CHOIR: Christ, have mercy upon us.

CANTOR: Lord, have mercy upon us.

[The Lord's Prayer and the following versicles and responses are intoned:]

CANTOR: Our Father,

CHOIR: who art in heaven,

hallowed be thy name.

Thy kingdom come.

Thy will be done,

on earth as it is in heaven.

Give us this day our daily bread,

and forgive us our trespasses

as we forgive those who trespass against us,

and lead us not into temptation,

but deliver us from evil. Amen. [from Matthew 6:9b–13]

CANTOR: Blessed art thou, Lord God of our fathers;

CHOIR: To be praised and glorified above all for ever.

CANTOR: Let us bless the Father, the Son, and the Holy Ghost;

CHOIR: To be praised and glorified above all forever.

CANTOR: Blessed art thou, Lord God of our fathers;

CHOIR: Let us praise him and magnify him forever.

CANTOR: Blessed art thou, O Lord, in the firmament of heaven;

CHOIR: To be praised and glorified above all forever.

CANTOR: The Almighty and merciful Lord guard us and give us his blessing.

CHOIR: Amen.

[The Confession and Absolution are spoken:]

READER: We confess

READER: and CHOIR: to God Almighty, the Father, The Son, and the Holy Ghost, that we have sinned in thought, word, and deed, through our own grievous fault. Wherefore we pray God to have mercy upon us.

Almighty God, have mercy upon us, forgive us all our sins and deliver us from all evil, confirm and strengthen us in all goodness, and bring us to life everlasting. Through Jesus Christ our Lord. Amen.

READER: May the almighty and merciful Lord grant unto us pardon and remission of all our sins, time for amendment of life, and the grace and comfort of the Holy Spirit.

CHOIR: Amen.

[The following versicles and responses are chanted:]

CANTOR: Wilt thou not turn again and quicken us;

CHOIR: That thy people may rejoice in thee?

CANTOR: O Lord, shew thy mercy upon us;

CHOIR: And grant us thy salvation.

CANTOR: Vouchsafe, O Lord, to keep us this night without sin;

CHOIR: O Lord, have mercy upon us, have mercy upon us.

CANTOR: O Lord, hear our prayer;

CHOIR: And let our cry come unto thee.

CANTOR: Let us pray.

[Two or more collects are intoned by the CANTOR. At least one collect addresses the liturgical season of the church. A collect may be said for the benefit of a loved one of a choir member. At least one of the following collects may be intoned:]

Visit, we beseech thee, O Lord, this place, and drive from it all the snares of the enemy; let thy holy angels dwell herein to preserve us in peace; and may thy blessing be upon us evermore; through Jesus Christ our Lord.

Or

Lighten our darkness, we beseech thee, O Lord; and by thy great mercy defend us from all perils and dangers of this night; for the love of thy only Son, our Saviour, Jesus Christ.

Or

O Lord Jesus Christ, Son of the living God, who at this evening hour didst rest in the sepulcher, and didst thereby sanctify the grave to be a bed of hope to thy people; Make us so to abound in sorrow for our sins, which were the cause of thy passion, that when our bodies lie in the dust, our souls may live with thee; who livest and reignest with the Father and the Holy Ghost, one God, world without end.

Or

Look down, O Lord, from thy heavenly throne, illuminate the darkness of this night with thy celestial brightness, and from the sons of light banish the deeds of darkness; through Jesus Christ our Lord.

Or

Be present, O merciful God, and protect us through the silent hours of this night, so that we who are wearied by the changes and chances of this fleeting world may repose upon thy eternal changelessness; through Jesus Christ our Lord.

CHOIR: Amen.

[An anthem is sung, appropriate to the season of the church year.]

[The final versicles and responses are sung. The choir uses a setting composed by Peter Hallock:]

CANTOR: We will lay us down in peace and take our rest:

CHOIR: For it is thou, Lord, only that makest us to dwell in safety.

CANTOR: The Lord be with you:

CHOIR: And with thy spirit.

CANTOR: Let us bless the Lord:

CHOIR: Thanks be to God.

[The closing blessing is spoken:]

READER: The almighty and merciful Lord, the Father, the Son, and the Holy Ghost, bless and preserve us.

CHOIR: Amen.

Appendix B

MUSICAL EXAMPLES

[Listen to the examples on the website www.prayerasnightfalls.com]

Example 1: The Office of Compline
(See appendix A)

* * *

Example 2: Psalms 134 and 4

Words: *The Book of Common Prayer* 1979
Music: Peter R. Hallock (b. 1924), engraved 1987

PSALM 134 (ANTIPHON)

Behold now, bless the LORD, all you servants of the LORD, *
   you that stand by night in the house of the LORD.

Lift up your hands in the holy place and bless the LORD; *
   the Lord who made heaven and earth bless you out of
   Zion.

PSALM 4

Answer me when I call, O God, defender of my cause; *
     you set me free when I am hard-pressed; have mercy on
     me and hear my prayer.
"You mortals, how long will you dishonor my glory; *
how long will you worship dumb idols and run after false
     gods?"
Know that the LORD does wonders for the faithful; *
     when I call upon the LORD, he will hear me.
Tremble, then, and do not sin; *
     speak to your heart in silence upon your bed.
Offer the appointed sacrifices *
     and put your trust in the LORD.
Many are saying, "Oh, that we might see better times!" *
     Lift up the light of your countenance upon us, O LORD.
You have put gladness in my heart, *
     more than when grain and wine and oil increase.
I lie down in peace; at once I fall asleep; *
     for only you, LORD, make me dwell in safety.

(ANTIPHON)

Behold now, bless the Lord, all you servants of the Lord, *
     you that stand by night in the house of the Lord.
Lift up your hands in the holy place and bless the Lord; *
     the Lord who made heaven and earth bless you out of
     Zion.

✳   ✳   ✳

Example 3: Psalm 91

Words: *The Book of Common Prayer* 1979
Music: Peter R. Hallock (b. 1924), engraved 1991

He who dwells in the shelter of the Most High, *
    abides under the shadow of the Almighty.

He shall say to the LORD, "You are my refuge and my
    stronghold, *
    my God in whom I put my trust."

He shall deliver you from the snare of the hunter *
    and from the deadly pestilence.

He shall cover you with his pinions, and you shall find
    refuge under his wings; *
    his faithfulness shall be a shield and buckler.

You shall not be afraid of any terror by night, *
    nor of the arrow that flies by day;

Of the plague that stalks in the darkness, *
    nor of the sickness that lays waste at mid-day.

A thousand shall fall at your side, and ten thousand at your
    right hand, *
    but it shall not come near you.

Your eyes have only to behold *
    to see the reward of the wicked.

Because you have made the LORD your refuge, *
    and the Most High your habitation,

There shall no evil happen to you, *
    neither shall any plague come near your dwelling.

For he shall give his angels charge over you, *
> to keep you in all your ways.

They shall bear you in their hands, *
> lest you dash your foot against a stone.

You shall tread upon the lion and the adder; *
> you shall trample the young lion and the serpent under your feet.

Because he is bound to me in love, therefore will I deliver him; *
> I will protect him, because he knows my Name.

He shall call upon me, and I will answer him; *
> I am with him in trouble; I will rescue him and bring him to honor.

With long life will I satisfy him, *
> and show him my salvation.

✳   ✳   ✳

Example 4: Dear Lord and Father of mankind

Words: John Greenleaf Whittier (1807–92), stanzas 12 and 16 from "The Brewing of Soma" (1872)
Music: M. Searle Wright (1918–2004), from *Ten Orisons*, ©1961

Dear Lord and Father of mankind,
Forgive our foolish ways!
Reclothe us in our rightful mind,
In purer lives thy service find,
In deeper rev'rence, praise.

Drop thy still dews of quietness,

Till all our strivings cease:

Take from our souls the strain and stress,

And let our ordered lives confess

The beauty of thy peace.

✳ ✳ ✳

Example 5: If we could shut the gate

Words: John Danyel (1564–1626), *Songs for the Lute, Viol, and Voice (1606)*,
no. 17 (originally "If I could shut the gate"), adapted by Peter R. Hallock
Music: Peter R. Hallock (b. 1924), 2008

If we could shut the gate against our thoughts

And keep out sorrow from within:

Or memory could cancel all misdeeds,

And we unthink our sin,

How free, how clear, how clean our hearts would lie,

Discharged of such grievous company.

Or were there other rooms within the heart,

That did not to our conscience join so near,

Where we might lodge our thoughts apart

That we might not their clam'rous crying hear,

What peace, what joy, what ease should we possess,

Freed from the chains, our soul's oppress.

O Saviour, who our refuge art,

Let thy mercies stand twixt them and us,

And be the wall to separate our hearts,

so that we at length repose us free:

that peace, and joy, and rest may be within,

And we remain divided from our sin.

✳ ✳ ✳

Example 6: Nunc dimittis

Words: Luke 2:29–32 (KJV), with *Gloria Patri.* Order of Compline, *The Book of Common Prayer . . . Proposed in 1928,* Church of England
Music: William Byrd (ca. 1540–1623), setting of the canticle Magnificat in Tonus Peregrinus (ninth psalm tone), adapted by Carl Crosier (b. 1945)

Lord, now lettest thou thy servant depart in peace: according to thy word.

For mine eyes have seen thy salvation.

Which thou hast prepared before the face of all people;

To be a light to lighten the gentiles, and to be the glory of thy people Israel.

Glory be to the Father, and to the Son, and to the Holy Ghost.

As it was in the beginning, is now, and ever shall be, world without end. Amen.

✳ ✳ ✳

Example 7: Nunc dimittis

Words: Luke 2:29–32 (KJV), with *Gloria Patri.* Order of Compline, *The Book of Common Prayer . . . Proposed in 1928*, Church of England
Music: Thomas Tallis (ca. 1505–85), setting of the canticle *Benedictus*, adapted by Peter R. Hallock (b. 1924)

Lord, now lettest thou thy servant depart in peace according to thy word.

For mine eyes have seen thy salvation.

Which thou hast prepared before the face of all people;

To be a light to lighten the gentiles, and to be the glory of thy people Israel.

Glory be to the Father, and to the Son, and to the Holy Ghost.

As it was in the beginning, is now, and ever shall be, world without end. Amen.

✳   ✳   ✳

Example 8: Christians, to the paschal victim (Victimae paschali laudes)

Words: Wigbert (Wipo of Burgundy) (died ca. 1050), trans. *The Antiphoner and Grail*, 1880. *The Hymnal 1982*
Music: sequence *Victimae paschali laudes*, Mode 1; melody attr. Wigbert (Wipo of Burgundy) (died ca. 1050)

Christians, to the Paschal victim
Offer your thankful praises!
A lamb the sheep redeemeth: Christ, who only is sinless,

Reconcileth sinners to the Father.

Death and life have contended

In that combat stupendous:

The Prince of life, who died, reigns immortal.

Speak, Mary, declaring

What thou sawest, wayfaring.

"The tomb of Christ, who is living,

The glory of Jesus' resurrection;

Bright angels attesting,

The shroud and napkin resting.

Yea, Christ my hope is arisen:

To Galilee he will go before you."

Christ indeed from death is risen,

Our new life obtaining.

Have mercy, victor King, ever reigning! Amen. Alleluia!

✳   ✳   ✳

Example 9: Bring us, O Lord, at our last awakening

Words: John Donne (1572–1631), from *A Sermon Preached at White-hall, February 29, 1628.* Rev. and ed. Eric Milner-White (1884–1964)
Music: Peter R. Hallock (b. 1924), 1991

Bring us, O Lord God, at our last awakening

Into the house and gate of heaven.

To enter that gate and dwell in that house,

Where there shall be no darkness nor dazzling, but one
    equal light;

No noise nor silence, but one equal music;

No fears nor hopes, but one equal possession;

No ends nor beginnings, but one equal eternity;

In the habitation of thy glory and dominion,

World without end, Amen.

✳ ✳ ✳

Example 10: Phos Hilaron

Words: "O Gracious Light (Phos hilaron)," from Evening Prayer II, *The Book of Common Prayer 1979*, adapted by Kevin Siegfried

Music: Kevin Siegfried (b. 1969)

O gracious Light,

pure brightness of the everliving Father in Heaven,

O Jesus Christ, holy and blessed!

Now as we come to the setting of the sun,

and our eyes behold the vesper light,

We sing your praises, O God: Father, Son, and Holy Spirit.

You are worthy at all times to be praised by happy voices,

O Son of God, O Giver of life,

and to be glorified through all the worlds.

O gracious Light,

pure brightness of the everliving Father in Heaven,

We sing your praises, O God: Father, Son, and Holy Spirit.

O gracious Light.

✳ ✳ ✳

Example 11: O Christ, you are both light and day

Words: Plainsong hymn *Christe, qui Lux es et dies*, 6th c., ver. *Hymnal 1982*
(stanzas 1–3) and Charles P. Price (stanza 5)
Music: *Christe, qui Lux es et dies*, plainsong, Mode 2, *Mailander Hymnen*, 15th c.

O Christ, you are both light and day,
You drive away the shadowed night;
As Daystar you precede the dawn,
The Herald of the light to come.

We pray you, O most holy Lord,
To be our guardian while we sleep;
Bestow on us who rest in you
The blessing of a quiet night.

Although our eyes in sleep be closed,
Let hearts in constant vigil watch;
With your right hand you will protect
Those who believe and trust in you.

O Christ, Redeemer of the world,
O God, our Maker and our end,
O Spirit, bond of peace and love,
To you be thanks and endless praise.

✳ ✳ ✳

Example 12: Psalm 139

Words: *The Book of Common Prayer 1979*
Music: Peter R. Hallock (b. 1924), written mid-1980s

LORD, you have searched me out and known me; *
> you know my sitting down and my rising up;
> you discern my thoughts from afar.
You trace my journeys and my resting-places *
> and are acquainted with all my ways.
Indeed, there is not a word on my lips, *
> but you, O LORD, know it altogether.
You press upon me behind and before *
> and lay your hand upon me.
Such knowledge is too wonderful for me; *
> it is so high that I cannot attain to it.
Where can I go then from your Spirit? *
> where can I flee from your presence?
If I climb up to heaven, you are there; *
> if I make the grave my bed, you are there also.
If I take the wings of the morning *
> and dwell in the uttermost parts of the sea,
Even there your hand will lead me *
> and your right hand hold me fast.
If I say, "Surely the darkness will cover me, *
> and the light around me turn to night,"
Darkness is not dark to you; *
> night is as bright as the day; *

darkness and light to you are both alike.

For you yourself created my inmost parts; *

you knit me together in my mother's womb.

I will thank you because I am marvelously made; *

your works are wonderful, and I know it well.

My body was not hidden from you, *

while I was being made in secret

and woven in the depths of the earth.

Your eyes beheld my limbs, yet unfinished in the womb;

all of them were written in your book; *

they were fashioned day by day,

when as yet there was none of them.

How deep I find your thoughts, O God! *

how great is the sum of them!

If I were to count them, they would be more in number

than the sand; *

to count them all, my life span would need to be like

yours.

Oh, that you would slay the wicked, O God! *

You that thirst for blood, depart from me.[140]

They speak despitefully against you; *

your enemies take your Name in vain.

Do I not hate those, O LORD, who hate you? *

and do I not loathe those who rise up against you?

I hate them with a perfect hatred; *

they have become my own enemies.

Search me out, O God, and know my heart; *

try me and know my restless thoughts.

Look well whether there be any wickedness in me *

and lead me in the way that is everlasting.

✳ ✳ ✳

Example 13: Slowly the rays of daylight fade

Words: Adelaide Anne Proctor (1825–62), third stanza of "An Evening Hymn," in *Legends and Lyrics*, second series (1860)
Music: M. Searle Wright (1918–2004), from *Ten Orisons*, ©1961

Slowly the rays of daylight fade:

So fade within our heart

The hopes in earthly love and joy,

That one by one depart.

Slowly the bright stars, one by one,

Within the heavens shine:

Give us, O Lord, fresh hopes in heav'n

And trust in things divine.

✳ ✳ ✳

Example 14: God be in my head

Words: *The English Primer of 1551*
Music: Douglas Fullington (b. 1969)

God be in my head, and in my understanding;

God be in mine eyes, and in my looking;

God be in my mouth, and in my speaking;

God be in my heart, and in my thinking;

God be at mine end, and at my departing.

✳   ✳   ✳

Example 15: Te lucis ante terminum

Words: Compline hymn *Te lucis ante terminum.* Latin verses 1 and 2 from Office of Compline, *Liber Usualis.* English verses 1, 2, and 4 from *The Hymnal 1982*

Music: plainsong, mode 8; polyphony by Kevin Siegfried (b. 1969)

Te lucis ante terminum,

Rerum Creator poscimus,

Ut pro tua clementia

Sis praesul et custodia.

To you before the close of day,

Creator of all things we pray

That in your constant clemency

Our guard and keeper you would be.

Procul recedant somnia,

Et noctium phantasmata;

Hostemque nostrum comprime,

Ne polluantur corpora.

Save us from troubled, restless sleep,

From all ill dreams your children keep;

So calm our minds that fears may cease

And rested bodies wake in peace.

Almighty Father, hear our cry

Through Jesus Christ, our Lord Most High,

Whom with the Spirit we adore

For ever and for evermore.

✳ ✳ ✳

Example 16: God is with us

Words: Byzantine rite, from Great Compline, translated by Archimandrite Ephrem Lash

Music: Mode Plagal 2, Petros Lampadarios (ca.1730–78)

God is with us, understand you nations, and submit.

> For God is with us.

To the ends of the earth give ear.

> For God is with us.

Submit, you mighty ones.

> For God is with us.

If again you become strong, you will also submit again.

> For God is with us.

And whatever you plan, the Lord will scatter it.

> For God is with us.

And whatever word you speak, it will not remain among you.

> For God is with us.

Fear of you we shall not fear, nor shall we be troubled.

> For God is with us.

The Lord our God, let us sanctify him, and he will be our fear.

> For God is with us.

And if I should trust in him, he will be sanctification for me.

> For God is with us.

And I will trust in him, and I will be saved through him.

> For God is with us.

Here am I and the children whom God has given me.

> For God is with us.

The people who walked in darkness have seen a great light.

> For God is with us.

We who dwell in the land and the shadow of death, a light will shine on us.

> For God is with us.

For unto us a Child is born, unto us a Son is given.

> For God is with us.

Whose government was upon his shoulder.

> For God is with us.

And of his peace there is no bound.

> For God is with us.

And his name shall be called, Angel of great counsel.

> For God is with us.

Wonderful Counsellor.

> For God is with us.

Mighty God, Ruler, Prince of peace.

For God is with us.

Father of the age to come.

For God is with us.

Glory to the Father and to the Son and to the Holy Spirit.

Both now and ever and to the ages of ages Amen.

God is with us, understand you nations, and submit

For God is with us.

✳ ✳ ✳

Example 17: Ave Rosa Sine Spinis

Words: anon., Marian Antiphon, trope of the beginning of the *Ave Maria*
Music: Thomas Tallis (ca. 1505–85), ca. 1540

Hail, rose without thorns, whom the father set on high in divine majesty and made free from all sorrow.

Mary, called the star of the sea, by your son you are made resplendent with the bright light of divinity, through which you shine with every virtue.

Full of grace the holy spirit filled you while it made you the vessel of divine goodness and total obedience.

The Lord is with you in a wondrous way, the word of life made flesh by the deed of the triune creator: Oh, how sweet a vessel of love.

Blessed are you among women: this is declared to all nations. The heavens acknowledge you to be blessed and raised high above all.

And blessed is the fruit of your womb, a gift for us always to enjoy here as an inner foretaste, and after death in perpetuity.

O merciful virgin Mary, receive into the holy refuge of your heart this perception of salvation, the grateful object of your prayers. Amen.

✳ ✳ ✳

Example 18: Sicut Cervus

Words: Psalm 42:1
Music: Giovanni Pierluigi da Palestrina (ca. 1525–94)

Sicut cervus desiderat ad fontes aquarum
Ita desiderat anima mea ad te, Deus.

English translation:
As the deer longs for the water-brooks
So longs my soul for you, O God.

✳ ✳ ✳

Example 19: To the Supreme Being

Words: Michelangelo Buonarroti (1475–1564), trans. William Wordsworth
(1770–1850), adapted by Peter R. Hallock (b. 1924), 1993
Music: Peter R. Hallock (b. 1924), 1993

The prayers we make will then be sweet indeed

If Thou the spirit give by which we pray.

Our unassisted hearts are barren clay,

Which of its native self can nothing feed:

Of good and pious works Thou art the seed,

Which quickens only when Thou say'st it may.

Unless Thou show to us Thine own true way—

No one can find it, Lord! Thou must lead.

Do thou, then, breathe those thoughts into our minds

By which such virtue may be bred,

That in thy holy footsteps we may tread.

The fetters of our tongues unbind,

That we may have the grace

By which our songs may rise to Thee

That we may sound thy praises everlastingly.

✳   ✳   ✳

Example 20: Lamentations

Words: Lamentations of Jeremiah 1:1–2
Music: Peter R. Hallock (b. 1924), 1972, ed. Carl Crosier, 1986

Here begins the Lamentation of Jeremiah the Prophet.

How deserted lies the city once so full of people: how like a widow she is, who once was great among the nations, and princess among the provinces, how is she become tributary.

Bitterly she weeps in the night, and tears are upon her cheeks:

Among all her lovers there is none to comfort her.

All of her friends have betrayed her; they have become her enemies.

Jerusalem, Jerusalem, return to the Lord your God.

✳   ✳   ✳

Example 21: Easter Canticle

Words: 1 Corinthians 5:7–8; Romans 6:9–11; 1 Corinthians 15:20–22
Music: Peter R. Hallock (b. 1924), 1970

Christ our Passover is sacrificed for us;

Therefore let us keep the feast,

Not with old leaven, neither with the leaven of malice and evil,

But with the unleavened bread of sincerity and truth.
Alleluia! Alleluia! Alleluia!

Christ being raised from the dead dieth no more;
Death hath no more dominion over him.
For in that he died, he died unto sin once:
But in that he liveth, he liveth unto God.
Likewise reckon yourselves to be dead indeed unto sin,
But alive unto God through Jesus Christ our Lord.
Alleluia! Alleluia! Alleluia!

Christ is risen from the dead,
And become the firstfruits of them that slept.
For since by man came death,
By man came also the resurrection of the dead.
For as in Adam all die,
Even so in Christ shall all be made alive.

Glory be to the Father, and to the Son, and to the Holy Ghost;
As it was in the beginning, is now and ever shall be,
World without end. Amen.
Alleluia! Alleluia! Alleluia!

✳ ✳ ✳

Example 22: Sometimes I feel like a motherless child

Words: American traditional spiritual
Music: American traditional spiritual, arranged by Brian Fairbanks (b. 1968)

Sometimes I feel like a motherless child,
A long way from home.

Sometimes I feel like I'm almost gone,
A long way from home.

✳ ✳ ✳

Example 23: Land of Rest

Words: Stanzas 1, 12, 22, 23, and 26 from a poem by "F. B. P." in a 17th-c. manuscript in the British Museum
Music: *Land of Rest*, American folk hymn adapted by Annabel Morris Buchanan (1889–1983), arranged for the Compline Choir by Richard T. Proulx (1937–2010)

Jerusalem, my happy home, when shall I come to thee?
When shall my sorrows have an end? Thy joys when shall
     I see?

Thy saints are crowned with glory great; they see God face
     to face;
They triumph still, they still rejoice: Most happy is their
     case.

There David stands with harp in hand as master of the
     choir:

Ten thousand times that man were blest that might this
music hear.

Our Lady sings Magnificat with tune surpassing sweet;
And all the virgins bear their part, sitting about her feet.

Jerusalem, Jerusalem, God grant that I may see
Thine endless joy, and of the same partaker ever be.

✳ ✳ ✳

Example 24: Salve Regina

Words and Music: Attributed to Hermann of Reichenau (1013–54)

Salve, Regina, mater misericordiae;
vita, dulcedo et spes nostra, salve.
Ad te clamamus, exules, filii Evae.
Ad te suspiramus, gementes et flentes
in hac lacrimarum valle.
Eia ergo, advocata nostra,
illos tuos misericordes oculos ad nos converte.
Et Iesum, benedictum fructum ventris tui,
nobis post hoc exsilium ostende.
O Clemens, O pia, O dulcis Virgo Maria.

English translation:
Hail, holy Queen, Mother of mercy,
hail, our life, our sweetness, and our hope.

To you we cry, the children of Eve;

to you we send up our sighs,

mourning and weeping in this land of exile.

Turn, then, most gracious advocate,

your eyes of mercy toward us;

lead us home at last

and show us the blessed fruit of your womb, Jesus:

O clement, O loving, O sweet virgin Mary.

*   *   *

Example 25: Now the day is over

Words: Sabine Baring-Gould (1834–1924). Stanzas 1, 3, and 6
Music: *Merrial,* by Sir Joseph Barnby (1838–96), 1868. *The Hymnal 1982*

Now the day is over,

Night is drawing nigh,

Shadows of the evening

Steal across the sky.

Jesus, give the weary

Calm and sweet repose;

With thy tend'rest blessing

May our eyelids close.

Through the long night watches

May thine angels spread

Their white wings above me,

Watching round my bed.

Appendix C

A SELECTED LIST OF RESOURCES
FOR PRAYING COMPLINE

Most of the resources where Compline or Night Prayer may be found are also sources for praying the Divine Hours. Printed resources for Compline or Night Prayer only have a comment to that effect, and those with an asterisk (*) contain musical notation for chanting. I apologize in advance for any omissions or errors in the list, but I will make an updated list available on www.prayerasnightfalls.com.

For those interested specifically in praying Morning and Evening Prayer, an excellent guide to printed resources, with commentary, is found in Paul Boers, *The Rhythm of God's Grace* (Brewster, MA: Paraclete Press, 2003). It includes some sources for Compline not listed below.

Online Websites for Praying Compline / Night Prayer

ANGLICAN CHURCH

http://justus.anglican.org/resources/bcp/bcp.htm

A gateway to online versions of the Book of Common

Prayer for various countries of the worldwide Anglican Communion.

http://www.churchofengland.org/prayer-worship/worship/texts/daily2.aspx

Church of England, *Common Worship.* Menu on left will link to Night Prayer in contemporary or traditional language.

COPTIC ORTHODOX CHURCH

www.agpeya.org

Links to an online Book of Hours for the Coptic Orthodox Church.

ORTHODOX CHURCH

http://www.anastasis.org.uk/small_compline.htm
http://www.anastasis.org.uk/great_compline.htm

Small Compline and Great Compline from the Byzantine Rite.

ROMAN CATHOLIC CHURCH—
LITURGY OF THE HOURS (1974)

www.divineoffice.org

Online Liturgy of the Hours, for today's date as well as the day before and after.

www.universalis.com

Gives the Liturgy of the Hours, as well as readings for Mass, for today's date as well as the day before and the week ahead. The Psalms are not the Grail versions for copyright reasons.

www.ebreviary.com

Viewable files in Adobe PDF format of the Liturgy of the Hours for various options (daily, weekly, monthly), based on free or subscription viewing.

ROMAN CATHOLIC CHURCH— OFFICIUM DIVINUM (PRE-1970)

www.divinumofficium.com

A free website for the *Officium Divinum.* Under "Ordo," one may use three different versions: 1570, Divino Afflatu (Pius X breviary), and 1960.

www.breviary.mobi/

Access to the *Officium Divinum* with a subscription donation. Site may also be accessed from www.breviary.net.

Printed Resources for Praying Compline / Night Prayer

ANGLICAN CHURCH

*Compline: An Order for Night Prayer in Traditional Language. Royal School of Church Music for the Plainsong and Medieval Music Society, 2005. This is the version of Compline sung in Seattle from the original publication

of 1949. The new version is based on the *Common Worship* version of Night Prayer in traditional language (2000) with the same music as the 1949 publication.

The Book of Common Prayer. New York: Church Hymnal Corporation and Seabury Press, 1979.

The Prayer Book Office. New York: The Church Hymnal Corporation, 1994.

Hour by Hour. Cincinnati: Forward Movement Publications, 2003.

An Order for Compline. Cincinnati: Forward Movement Publications, 2003. Compline only.

A New Zealand Prayer Book: He Karakia Mihinare o Aotearoa. London/Auckland: Collins, 1989; San Francisco: HarperSanFrancisco, 1997.

Night Prayer (Compline) and *Night Prayer (Compline) in Traditional Language.* London: Church House Publishing, 2000. Compline only. These are the official publications from *Common Worship: Services and Prayers for the Church of England.*

The Anglican Breviary. Frank Gavin Liturgical Foundation, 1955, reprinted 1998. A complete English translation of the Roman Breviary before Vatican II.

LUTHERAN CHURCH

Lutheran Book of Worship. Minneapolis and Philadelphia: Augsburg Publishing House and Board of Publication, Lutheran Church in America, 1978.

Evangelical Lutheran Worship. Minneapolis: Augsburg Fortress, 2006.

For All the Saints: Prayer Book For and By the Church. Delhi, NY: American Lutheran Publicity Bureau, 1996.

COPTIC ORTHODOX CHURCH

The Agpeya: The Book of Hours in the Coptic Rite. Coptic Orthodox Diocese of Los Angeles, Southern California, and Hawaii, 2010. Kindle Edition

ORTHODOX CHURCH

Holy Transfiguration Monastery, trans. *A Prayer Book for Orthodox Christians.* Haverhill, MA: The Holy Transfiguration Monastery, 2005. Includes Small Compline.

PRESBYTERIAN

Book of Common Worship. Louisville: Westminster John Knox, 1993. Section "Daily Prayer."

ROMAN CATHOLIC CHURCH— LITURGY OF THE HOURS (1974)

*The Office of Compline: In Latin and English. San Francisco: Ignatius, 2010. Compline only. From the St. Louis Antiphonary of the Hours.

The Liturgy of the Hours. New York: Catholic Book Publishing Company, 1975. A four-volume set containing all seven offices.

Christian Prayer: The Liturgy of the Hours. New York: Catholic Book Publishing Company, 1976. A single-volume condensation containing Morning, Evening, and Night Prayer, and a selection from the other offices.

Shorter Christian Prayer. New York: Catholic Book Publishing Company, 1998. The basic four-week cycle of prayer only, but ideal for traveling.

Nugent, Madeline Pecora. *The Divine Office for Dodos (*Devout, Obedient Disciples of Our Savior).* New Jersey: Catholic Book Publishing, 2008. A complete how-to-use guide for the Liturgy of the Hours, with principles that could be applied to any breviary.

ROMAN CATHOLIC CHURCH—
OFFICIUM DIVINUM (PRE-1970)

*Ad Completorium: The Rite of Compline for Every Day of the Liturgical Year According to the Roman Breviary of 1960. London: Saint Austin Press, 2000. Compline only, with chant.

*Both the *Antiphonale Romanum* (1912) and the *Liber Usualis* (1961) are among the vast number of resources that can be downloaded from the site Musica Sacra: The Church Music Association of America, at http://musicasacra.com/communio/.

UNITED METHODIST CHURCH
The Book of Offices and Services. Akron, OH: Order of Saint Luke, 1994.

GENERAL COLLECTIONS CONTAINING
COMPLINE/NIGHT PRAYER

Adam, David. *The Rhythm of Life: Celtic Daily Prayer.* Harrisburg, PA: Morehouse, 1996.

Benson, Robert. *Venite: A Book of Daily Prayer.* New York: Tarcher/Putnam, 2000. A book of daily prayer is also included in the collection *Daily Prayer: A Simple Plan for Learning to Say the Daily Prayer of the Church.* Raleigh, NC: Carolina Broadcasting and Publishing, 2006. Includes CD and DVD.

Carmelites of Indianapolis. *People's Companion to the Breviary.* 2 vols. Indianapolis: Carmelites of Indianapolis, 1997.

Community of Jesus. *The Little Book of Hours: Praying with the Community of Jesus.* Brewster, MA: Paraclete Press, 2007.

Cotter, Jim. *Prayer at Night's Approaching.* Harrisburg, PA: Morehouse, 1983, 1991, 1997.

Glenstal Abbey. *The Glenstal Book of Prayer: A Benedictine Prayer Book.* Collegeville, MN: Liturgical Press, 2001.

Hamilton, Lisa B. *Daily Prayer for Times of Grief.* Brewster, MA: Paraclete Press, 2001.

Northumbria Community. *Celtic Daily Prayer: Prayers and Readings from the Northumbria Community.* New York: HarperCollins, 2002. Contains *Celtic Daily Prayer* (1994) and *Celtic Night Prayer* (1996).

Society of St. Francis. *Celebrating Common Prayer.* New York: Mowbray, 1992.

Storey, William G. *An Everyday Book of Hours.* Chicago: Liturgical Training Publications, 2001.

Sutera, Judith, ed. *Work of God.* Collegeville, MN: Liturgical Press, 1997.

Tickle, Phyllis A. *The Divine Hours.* 3 vols.: *Prayers for Summertime, Prayers for Autumn and Winter,* and *Prayers for Spring.* New York: Doubleday, 2000–2001.

Webber, Robert, ed. *The Prymer: The Prayer Book of the Medieval Era Adapted for Contemporary Use.* Brewster, MA: Paraclete Press, 2000.

Wiederkehr, Macrina. *Seven Sacred Pauses: Living Mindfully Through the Hours of the Day.* Notre Dame: Sorin Books, 2008. Companion CD: Frye, Velma. *Seven Sacred Pauses: Singing Mindfully Dawn Through Dark.* Velma Frye Music, 2007.

BOOKS ABOUT THE DIVINE HOURS, CHANT, AND MONASTIC SPIRITUALITY

Benson, Robert. *In Constant Prayer.* Nashville: Thomas Nelson, 2008.

Boers, Arthur Paul. *The Rhythm of God's Grace.* Brewster, MA: Paraclete Press, 2003.

Bourgeault, Cynthia. *Chanting the Psalms: A Practical Guide with Instructional CD.* Boston: New Seeds, 2006.

Community of Jesus. *The Song of Prayer: A Practical Guide to Learning Gregorian Chant.* Brewster, MA: Paraclete Press, 2010.

McKnight, Scot. *Praying with the Church: Following Jesus Daily, Hourly, Today.* Brewster, MA: Paraclete Press, 2006.

Norris, Kathleen. *The Cloister Walk.* New York: Riverhead, 1996.

Steindl-Rast, David, and Sharon Lebell. *Music of Silence: A Sacred Journey Through the Hours of the Day.* Foreword by Kathleen Norris. Berkeley, CA: Seastone, 1998.

Wiederkehr, Macrina. *Seven Sacred Pauses: Living Mindfully Through the Hours of the Day.* Notre Dame: Sorin Books, 2008.

Notes

1 ✳ Compline in the Holy Box
AN INTRODUCTION

1   Edmond Browning, former presiding bishop of the Episcopal Church USA, excerpt from closing paragraphs of an address to the Executive Council, diocese of Olympia, in Bellevue, Washington, June 13, 1995.

2   Ps. 50(51):16. See note 12 about the numbering of psalms.

3   The interesting history of the building can be found in *The Holy Box: The Story of St. Mark's Cathedral*, by the Very Rev. John C. Leffler, dean of St. Mark's Episcopal Cathedral from 1951–1971.

4   The *Lutheran Book of Worship* (Minneapolis and Philadelphia: Augsburg Publishing House and Board of Publication, Lutheran Church in America, 1978), and the *Book of Common Prayer 1979* (New York: Church Hymnal Corporation and Seabury Press, 1979). Several events held in Seattle during the 1970s, such as the General Convention of the Episcopal Church and the National Convention of the American Guild of Organists, produced large gatherings at Compline and did much to communicate its appeal.

5   Because some people bring their own blankets, an Internet "Mystery Worshipper" named it "God's slumber party." See "St Mark's Cathedral, Seattle, Washington, USA," *Ship of Fools*, http://www.shipoffools.com/mystery/2007/1384.html, and also "The Faithful Are Casual at This Sunday Service," *New York Times*, March 16, 1997, 16.

6   The service is broadcast by KING-FM (98.1) from Seattle, and streamed over www.king.org. The Compline Choir also produces podcasts of the service, which are available at www.complinechoir.org.

7   One of the characteristics of the "Emerging Church" is the engagement of once-separate branches of Christianity, such as the "evangelicals" and "liturgicals"; this has resulted in a reconnection of many with "ancient practices" like fixed-hour prayer. See Phyllis Tickle, *The Great Emergence: How Christianity is Changing and Why* (Grand Rapids: Baker, 2008), 133.

8   Peter Hallock, "The 'It' of Compline," *Saint Mark's Cathedral Rubric* (January 22, 1984).

2 ✳ Round Me Falls the Night
ELEMENTS OF COMPLINE

9   Paul Gerhardt, in *Praxis Pietatis Melica*, ed. Johann Crüger, 3rd ed. (1648) (*Nun ruhen alle Wälder*); paraphrased by Robert S. Bridges, 1899.

10   See the books listed in the last section of appendix C.

11   See David Steindl-Rast and Sharon Lebell, *Music of Silence: A Sacred Journey Through the Hours of the Day* (Berkeley, CA: Seastone, 1998), 3–4.

12   Psalms are given as two numbers when the numbers differ between the systems based on the Greek Septuagint (left side) and Hebrew (right side). The latter numbering is used in most Bibles and prayer books today, but the Greek system is used in many publications, especially older books of chant.

3 ✳ At Day's Close
NIGHT IN ANCIENT TIMES

13   Geoffrey Keynes, ed., *The Works of Sir Thomas Browne* (London, 1931), 3:230.

14   Jean Verdon, *Night in the Middle Ages* (Notre Dame: University of Notre Dame Press, 2002), 50.

15   For more about these concerns, see A. Roger Ekirch, *At Day's Close: Night in Times Past* (New York: W. W. Norton, 2005), 14, 59–60, 97.

16 *Rudens,* by Titus Marcius Plautus (254–184 BC).

17 Diana L. Eck, *Darsan: Seeing the Divine Image in India* (New York: Columbia University Press, 1996), 47–48.

18 Many of the laws of Judaism were collected in the Mishnah ("repetition") in the period from the destruction of the temple in AD 70 to about 220. Over the next three centuries, rabbinic commentaries were added, forming the Talmud.

19 Deut. 6:4–9. Unless otherwise noted, all Scripture citations are from *The Holy Bible: New Revised Standard Edition* (New York: Collins, 1989).

20 For the following discussion I consulted *The Complete ArtScroll Siddur: Weekday/Sabbath/Festival,* trans. Rabbi Nosson Scherman (New York: Mesorah, 1985), 318–25.

21 See note 12 about the numbering of psalms.

4 ✳ Be Sober, Be Vigilant
DARKNESS AND LIGHT

22 *An Order for Compline* (London: Plainsong and Medieval Music Society, 1949), 8.

23 Paraphrase of 1 Pet. 5:8–9.

24 See note 12 for the numbering of psalms.

25 Ps. 91:5–6 (*Book of Common Prayer 1979*).

26 Wayne Teasdale, *The Mystic Hours: A Daybook of Interspiritual Wisdom and Devotion* (Novato, CA: New World Library, 2004), reading no. 348.

27 Rom. 7:16, 18b.

28 Ps. 4:4 (*Book of Common Prayer 1979*).

29 John Greenleaf Whittier, "The Brewing of Soma" (1872), stanzas 12 and 16.

30 John Danyel (1564–1626), *Songs for the Lute, Viol, and Voice (1606),* no. 17 (originally "If I could shut the gate"), adapted by Peter Hallock for the Compline Choir as "If we could shut the gate" (2008), stanza 1.

31 "If we could shut the gate," stanza 3.

32   This is one of the Gospel canticles——see chap. 2.

33   Lk. 2:29–32. From Prayer at the Close of the Day: Compline, *Lutheran Book of Worship*, 159.

34   Lk. 2:36–38.

35   Harvey Cox, *When Jesus Came to Harvard: Making Moral Choices Today* (Boston: Houghton Mifflin, 2004), 87.

36   James Finley, *Merton's Palace of Nowhere: A Search for God through Awareness of the True Self* (Notre Dame: Ave Maria Press, 1978), 103.

37   Robert Johnson, *Transformation: Understanding Three Levels of Masculine Consciousness* (New York: HarperCollins, 1991), 55.

38   Ps. 139:12 (*Book of Common Prayer 1979*).

5 ✳ A Quiet Night and a Perfect End
DEATH AND LIFE

39   *The Book of Common Prayer: With the Additions and Deviations Proposed in 1928* (London: SPCK, 1928), 352.

40   Christine Longaker, *Facing Death and Finding Hope: A Guide to the Emotional and Spiritual Care of the Dying* (New York: Doubleday, 1997), 113.

41   The *Dies Irae*, perhaps the best known of the sequences, was used in the Masses for the Dead until 1970, but is still sung in the Tridentine Requiem Mass.

42   On Easter, we sing it instead of the hymn at Compline. In the Roman Catholic Church, it is appointed for all the Masses during Easter Week.

43   Latin text is from *The Gregorian Missal for Sundays* (Solesmes: St. Peter's Abbey, 1990), 351–53; English translation is from *The Hymnal 1982* (New York: Church Hymnal Corporation, 1985), no. 183.

44   For two examples of recent views on the resurrection, see John Shelby Spong, *Jesus for the Non-Religious* (New York: HarperCollins, 2007), 117–18, and Gary R. Habermas, *The Risen Jesus and Future Hope* (Lanham, MD: Rowman & Littlefield, 2003) 9–10.

45   Fr. Francis Tiso, associate director for the Secretariat for

Ecumenical and Interreligious Affairs, United States Conference of Catholic Bishops, from 2004 to 2009, went to the village of Khenpo A-chos in 2000, and made tape-recorded testimony of four witnesses. For further details, see Gail Holland, "Christian Buddhist Explorations: The Rainbow Body," *IONS Review* 59 (March-May 2002); also an interview with Fr. Tiso: "Christ in Buddha Nature: Two Worlds——One Heart," October 15, 2001, www.newdimensions.org.

46 Thomas Traherne (1637–1674), quoted in Andrew Harvey, ed., *The Essential Mystics* (New York: Castle, 1996), 207.

47 Charles Wesley (1707–1788), hymn "Love divine, all love's excelling."

48 Alan Watts, *The Wisdom of Insecurity* (New York: Vintage, 1951), 152.

49 John Donne, "A Sermon Preached at White-hall, February 29, 1627 [1627/8]," in *The Sermons of John Donne*, vol. 8, no. 7, ed. E. M. S. Simpson and G. R. Potter (Berkeley: University of California Press, 1956; digital publisher Brigham Young University, 2004–5).

50 Ibid., 1.

51 Ibid., 18. The quotation "Surely the Lord is in this place . . ." comes from Gen. 28:16–17.

6 ✳ Before the Ending of the Day
CHRISTIAN ORIGINS OF COMPLINE

52 *An Order for Compline* (London: Plainsong and Medieval Music Society, 1949), 8.

53 Robert Taft, *The Liturgy of the Hours in East and West* (Collegeville, MN: Liturgical Press, 1993), 7.

54 Ibid., 9. Acts 2:15; 3:1; 10:3, 9 30, refers to prayer at the third, sixth, and ninth hours, respectively.

55 Ibid., 13.

56 Ibid., 14–16.

57 Quoted in Paul F. Bradshaw, *Daily Prayer in the Early Church* (New York: Oxford University Press, 1982), 54.

58 Quoted in ibid., 52.

59 *Book of Common Prayer 1979*, 112.

60 Taft, *The Liturgy of the Hours in East and West*, 86.

61 Ibid., 94.

62 Given in ibid., 123 and 138.

63 Timothy Fry, ed., *RB 1980: The Rule of St. Benedict* (Collegeville, MN: Liturgical Press, 1980), 17:9–10 (p. 213).

64 Ibid., 18.19 (p. 215). Note that Pss. 90 and 133 are equivalent to 91 and 134 in the Hebrew numbering; see note 12.

65 Translation from *The Episcopal Hymnal 1982*, hymn number 40, first stanza.

66 Peter Jeffrey, "Eastern and Western Elements in the Irish Monastic Prayer of the Hours," in *The Divine Office in the Latin Middle Ages*, ed. Margot E. Fassler and Rebecca A. Baltzer (Oxford: Oxford University Press, 2000), 118.

67 See *The Antiphonary of Bangor*, ed. F. E. Warren (London: Harrison and Sons, 1895), part 2, 21, no. 33. The translation was made by Bill McJohn.

7 ✳ Seeking God Seeking Me
COMPLINE AND THE MYSTIC PATH

68 Rainer Maria Rilke, "I love the dark hours of my being," in *Rilke's Book of Hours: Love Poems to God*, trans. Anita Barrows and Joanna Macy (New York: Riverhead, 1996), 51.

69 Marilyn Ferguson, *The Aquarian Conspiracy: Personal and Social Transformation in Our Time* (Los Angeles: J. P. Tarcher, 1980, foreword/afterword, 1987), 363.

70 Rami Shapiro, *Minyan:The Ten Principles for Living a Life of Integrity* (New York: Crown, 1997), 193.

71 Teasdale, *The Mystic Hours*, reading no. 46.

72 Ps. 139:1–6, 10–11 (*Book of Common Prayer 1979*). See note 12 about the numbering of psalms.

73 See John Gorsuch, *An Invitation to the Spiritual Journey* (Mahwah, NJ: Paulist Press, 1990), 19–31.

74 Meizumi Roshi, quoted in Robert A. Johnson, *Transformation* (New York: HarperCollins, 1991), 84.

75 Gorsuch, *An Invitation to the Spiritual Journey*, 69–71.

76 James Finley, *Merton's Palace of Nowhere: A Search for God through Awareness of the True Self* (Notre Dame: Ave Maria Press, 1978), 82–83.

77 Gorsuch, *An Invitation to the Spiritual Journey*, 58.

78 See Andrew Harvey, *The Direct Path* (New York: Broadway, 2000), ix–x.

79 Timothy Fry, ed., *RB 1980: The Rule of St. Benedict in Latin and English with Notes* (Collegeville, MN: Liturgical Press, 1981), prologue:1 (p. 157).

80 Christopher Jamison, *Finding Sanctuary: Monastic Steps for Everyday Life* (Collegeville, MN: Liturgical Press, 2006), 76.

81 Cynthia Bourgeault, *Chanting the Psalms: A Practical Guide with Instructional CD* (Boston: New Seeds, 2006), 32–37.

82 An excellent guide to *lectio divina* is Christine Valters Paintner and Lucy Wynkoop, OSB, *Lectio Divina: Contemplative Awakening and Awareness* (Mahwah, NJ: Paulist Press, 2008).

8 ✳ From Canterbury to Constantinople
COMPLINE FROM 600 TO 1600

83 Compline hymn, *Christe, qui, splendor et dies*, in *The Office of Compline: Latin and English* (San Francisco: Ignatius, 2010), 109.

84 Diarmaid MacCulloch, *Christianity: The First Three Thousand Years* (New York: Penguin, 2009), 354.

85 These include the Armenian, Assyro-Chaldean, West-Syrian, Maronite, Coptic, and Ethiopian traditions. See separate discussions in Robert Taft, *The Liturgy of the Hours in East and West* (Collegeville, MN: Liturgical Press, 1993).

86 Pierre Salmon, *The Breviary Through the Centuries*, trans. Sr. David Mary, SNJM (Collegeville, MN: Liturgical Press, 1962), 12.

87 Contents are based on a generic "Hypertext Book of Hours," using texts from the *English Primer of 1599*, which can be found at http://medievalist.net/hourstxt/home.htm.

88 Frank L. Harrison, *Music in Medieval Britain* (London: Routledge and Kegan Paul, 1958), 81–82.

89 Based on *The Sarum Rite: Breviarium Sarisburiense cum nota, Psalterium: Ad completorium*, ed. William Renwick (Dundas, ON: Gregorian Institute of Canada, 2007), Tome A, Fascicule 2:359–406. Distributed over the Internet through .pdf files located at http://www.sarum-chant.ca.

9 ✳ To the Supreme Being
BEAUTY

90 Translated by William Wordsworth as "To the Supreme Being," in *The Complete Poetical Works* (London: Macmillan, 1888). Text altered by Peter Hallock.

91 St. Thomas Aquinas, *Summa Theologica: First Complete American Edition* (New York: Benzinger Brothers, 1947), 1:26 (Q.5, art. 4).

92 Elaine Scarry, *On Beauty and Being Just* (Princeton: Princeton University Press, 1999), 3–5, 23–25.

93 Ibid. 86–90.

94 Frank Burch Brown, *Good Taste, Bad Taste, and Christian Taste: Aesthetics in Religious Life* (New York: Oxford University Press, 2000), 13–25.

95 Robert M. Pirsig, *Zen and the Art of Motorcycle Maintenance* (New York: Bantam, 1974), 272.

96 Ibid., 221–22.

97 Ibid., 231.

98 Joan Chittister, *Illuminated Life: Monastic Wisdom for Seekers of Light* (Maryknoll, NY: Orbis, 2000), 29.

99 Paul Tillich, *The Protestant Era* (Chicago: University of Chicago Press, 1948), 59.

100 I'm thinking here of music that elicits a similar emotional response to "easy-listening" music on the radio. Brown, *Good Taste,*

Bad Taste, and Christian Taste, 251, speaks to this in one of twelve assumptions in the exercise of Christian taste in the arts: "While relative accessibility is imperative for most church art, the church also needs art . . . that continually challenges and solicits spiritual and theological growth in the aesthetic dimension. This is art that the Christian can grow into but seldom out of."

101 Ibid., 247.

102 See Jason Allen Anderson, "The Life and Works of Peter R. Hallock (b. 1924)" (Doctor of Musical Arts diss., University of Washington, 2007), 9–22. Dr. Anderson is currently director of the Compline Choir.

103 Ray W. Urwin, "An interview with Peter Hallock," *Journal of the Association of Anglican Musicians* (September 1992): 7.

104 Matthew Fox, *The Coming of the Cosmic Christ* (San Francisco: Harper & Row, 1988), 47–67.

10 ✳ Old Wine in New Bottles
COMPLINE FROM 1600 TO THE PRESENT

105 Last stanza of Compline hymn, *The Garden of the Soul* (London, 1775), 134.

106 Salmon, *The Breviary Through the Centuries,* 117.

107 See a translation of *Tra Le Sollecitudini* at *Adoremus Bulletin,* http://www.adoremus.org/TraLeSollecitudini.html.

108 In the 1920s and 1930s, Compline was sung, along with Vespers and Benediction of the Blessed Sacrament, at St. James Cathedral in Seattle. Compline and Benediction were done regularly on Sunday evenings in the 1930s, with various "ensembles of the men's and boys' choirs." The office was even broadcast on the radio during the early 1930s. See Clint Michael Kraus, "Music and Musicians at St. James Cathedral, Seattle, 1903–1953: The First 50 Years" (diss., University of Washington, 2009), 100.

109 For instance, the *Nunc Dimittis* was never a part of Compline in the Benedictine Order.

110 *The Garden of the Soul: Or, A Manual of Spiritual Exercises and Instructions* . . . (London, 1775), 130–36.

111 Reverend Thomas J. Williams, "Anglican Versions of the Breviary," *Project Canterbury* http://anglicanhistory.org/misc/breviary.html. The *Tracts of the Times* may also be found at the Project Canterbury site, http://www.anglicanhistory.org.

112 There were some wonderful exceptions, however. I sang often in the 1970s and 1980s with the choir *Cantores in Ecclesia* in Portland, Oregon, who sing Mass every Saturday evening. Now they sing both the Mass Ordinary (*Novus Ordo*) and the Mass Extraordinary (The Tridentine Mass).

113 The names have been changed as follows: Matins is now the Office of Readings; Lauds is Morning Prayer; Terce, Sext, and None are now Midmorning, Midday, and Midafternoon Prayer; Vespers and Compline are Evening Prayer and Night Prayer.

114 See Night Prayer in one of the four volumes of *The Liturgy of the Hours* (New York: Catholic Book Publishing Company, 1975), 6:636.

115 St. James Cathedral had a major renovation in 1994, and its acoustics have been marvelously restored.

116 The *Lutheran Book of Worship* (Mineapolis and Philadelphia: Augsburg Publishing House and Board of Publication, Lutheran Church in America, 1978), 154–60, and *The Book of Common Prayer* (New York: Church Hymnal Corporation, 1979), 127–35.

117 Marion Hatchett writes that the Song of Simeon is "suitably placed near the close of the rite." See Marion J. Hatchett, *Commentary on the American Prayer Book* (New York: Seabury, 1980), 147.

118 For further information on this and other publications mentioned, see appendix C.

119 It should be mentioned in this regard that Pope Benedict XVI, in 2011 (*Motu Proprio, Universe Ecclesiae*) sanctioned the use of the pre-1960 Breviary.

120 Robert Benson, *Venite: A Book of Daily Prayer* (New York: Tarcher/Putnam, 2000), 5.

11 ✳ The Monks of Broadway
COMMUNITY

121 Joan D. Chittister, OSB, *Wisdom Distilled from the Daily: Living the Rule of St. Benedict Today* (San Francisco: HarperSanFrancisco, 1990), 49.

122 M. Scott Peck, *The Different Drum: Community Making and Peace*, 2nd ed. (New York: Simon & Schuster, 1998), 137.

123 Joan D. Chittister, *The Rule of Benedict: Insights for the Ages* (New York: Crossroad, 1992), 36–37.

124 Quoted in Wayne Teasdale, *The Mystic Hours: A Daybook of Interspiritual Wisdom and Devotion* (Novato, CA: New World Library, 2004), reading no. 233.

125 Chittister, *The Rule of Benedict*, 35.

126 Thomas Merton, quoted in Teasdale, *The Mystic Hours*, reading no. 97.

127 Chittister, *The Rule of Benedict*, 50.

128 Timothy Fry, ed., *RB 1980: The Rule of St. Benedict in Latin and English with Notes* (Collegeville, MN: Liturgical Press, 1981), chap. 53.

12 ✳ In the Shadow of Your Wings
FINDING LASTING PEACE

129 *An Order for Compline* (London: Plainsong and Medieval Music Society, 1949), 12.

130 Ps. 91:1–4, 14 (*Book of Common Prayer 1979*).

131 Lauren Artress, *Walking a Sacred Path: Rediscovering the Labyrinth as a Spiritual Tool* (New York: Riverhead, 1995), 52.

132 Artress, *Walking a Sacred Path*, 65.

133 *Book of Common Prayer 1979*, 133.

134 Words are by Athelstan Riley (1858–1945).

135 David Steindl-Rast and Sharon Lebell, *Music of Silence: A Sacred Journey Through the Hours of the Day* (Berkeley, CA: Seastone, 1998), 112.

136 Ibid., 113.

137 Ibid., 112–13.

138 Carl Jung, "An Answer to Job," in *The Essential Jung*, ed. Anthony Storr (Princeton: Princeton University Press, 1983), 321–29.

139 Andrew Harvey and Anne Baring, *The Divine Feminine: Exploring the Feminine Face of God Throughout the World* (Berkeley: Conari, 1996), 182.

Appendix B

140 An alternate translation to these words of violence can be found in Nan C. Merrill, *Psalms for Praying: An Invitation to Wholeness* (New York: Continuum, 1999). "O that You would vanquish my fears, Beloved; O that ignorance and suffering would depart from me— All that separates me from true abandonment, to surrendering myself into your Hands!"

ABOUT PARACLETE PRESS

Who We Are

Paraclete Press is a publisher of books, recordings, and DVDs on Christian spirituality. Our publishing represents a full expression of Christian belief and practice—from Catholic to Evangelical, from Protestant to Orthodox.

We are the publishing arm of the Community of Jesus, an ecumenical monastic community in the Benedictine tradition. As such, we are uniquely positioned in the marketplace without connection to a large corporation and with informal relationships to many branches and denominations of faith.

What We Are Doing

BOOKS Paraclete publishes books that show the richness and depth of what it means to be Christian. Although Benedictine spirituality is at the heart of all that we do, we publish books that reflect the Christian experience across many cultures, time periods, and houses of worship. We publish books that nourish the vibrant life of the church and its people—books about spiritual practice, formation, history, ideas, and customs.

We have several different series, including the best-selling Paraclete Essentials and Paraclete Giants series of classic texts in contemporary English; Voices from the Monastery—men and women monastics writing about living a spiritual life today; award-winning poetry; best-selling gift books for children on the occasions of baptism and first communion; and the Active Prayer Series that brings creativity and liveliness to any life of prayer.

RECORDINGS From Gregorian chant to contemporary American choral works, our music recordings celebrate sacred choral music through the centuries. Paraclete distributes the recordings of the internationally acclaimed choir Gloriæ Dei Cantores, praised for their "rapt and fathomless spiritual intensity" by *American Record Guide*, and the Gloriæ Dei Cantores Schola, which specializes in the study and performance of Gregorian chant. Paraclete is also the exclusive North American distributor of the recordings of the Monastic Choir of St. Peter's Abbey in Solesmes, France, long considered to be a leading authority on Gregorian chant.

VIDEOS Our videos offer spiritual help, healing, and biblical guidance for life issues: grief and loss, marriage, forgiveness, anger management, facing death, and spiritual formation.

Learn more about us at our website: www.paracletepress.com, or call us toll-free at 1-800-451-5006.

SCAN TO READ MORE

YOU MAY ALSO BE INTERESTED IN

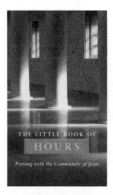

The Little Book of Hours

ISBN: 978-1-55725-533-4
$16.99 Paperback

Experience the depth and beauty of an ancient prayer practice as it is celebrated in a modern monastic community

At the Church of the Transfiguration on Cape Cod, the Liturgy of the Hours is observed each day by the Community of Jesus, an ecumenical Christian community in the Benedictine monastic tradition. In this little book, all the richness of these ancient prayers is presented in a modified version for Christians everywhere. *The Little Book of Hours* provides four weeks of services, with three services for every day, and many additional collects and services. Learn how you can "pray the hours" in the midst of your busy life today.

The Song of Prayer
A Practical Guide to Learning Gregorian Chant

ISBN: 978-1-55725-576-1
$21.99, Paperback plus CD

The Song of Prayer is the perfect introduction for those new to Gregorian chant and eager to learn about this profound way of prayer. Developed at the Community of Jesus where the Divine Office is sung in Latin every day, *The Song of Prayer* shows how chant takes Christians back to the early days of the church when people gathered together to pray each day, every day. You don't have to be highly musical in order to get started. An instructional 45-minute CD accompanies the book and provides a supreme example of the complete service of Compline, making learning easy and practical.

Available from most booksellers or through Paraclete Press:
www.paracletepress.com • 1-800-451-5006
Try your local bookstore first.